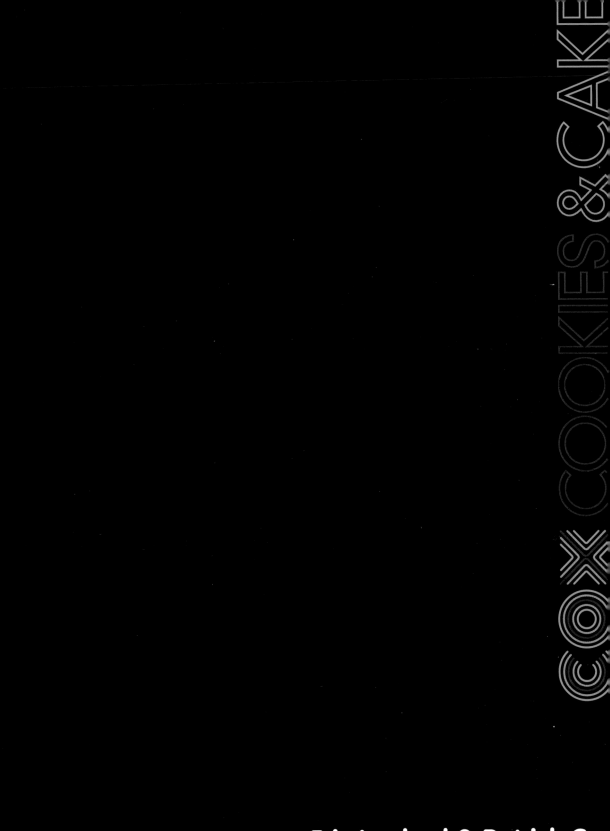

COX COOKIES & CAKE

Eric Lanlard & Patrick Cox

COX COOKIES & CAKE

Eric Lanlard & Patrick Cox

First published in 2011 by Mitchell Beazley, an imprint of Octopus Publishing Group Ltd,
Endeavour House, 189 Shaftesbury Avenue, London WC2H 8JY
www.octopusbooks.co.uk

An Hachette UK Company
www.hachette.co.uk

British Library Cataloguing-in-Publication Data.
A catalogue record for this book is available from the British Library.

Commissioning editor Becca Spry
Senior editor Sybella Stephens
Copy editor Lewis Esson
Proofreader Hilaire Walden
Indexer Ingrid Lock
Home economist Rachel Wood
Prop stylist Dawn Weller

Art director Jonathan Christie
Design & art direction Juliette Norsworthy
Photography Patrick Llewelyn-Davies (cover and recipes)
Photography Johnnie Shand Kydd (inside cover and pages 6, 8, 10, 36, 54, 72, 86, 122, 136)

Production manager Peter Hunt

ISBN: 978 1 84533 644 8
Printed and bound in China

All recipes have been tested in metric.
Muffin-size cupcake tins and standard muffin paper cases should be used for all cupcake
recipes, unless otherwise stated.
Medium eggs should be used, unless otherwise stated.
Whole milk should be used, unless otherwise stated.

CONTENTS

It was with a huge sense of wonderment and excitement when we first walked into the original Patrick Cox boutique on Symons Street in London. A velvet rope held back a wild throng of fashionistas, desperate to get their hands on a pair of his oh-so-hip Wannabe loafers. Cox's mad creativity and love of British irony transported the humble slip-on loafer and rocked it to the highest of heights. Mad candy colours, diamante embellishments, exotic animal skins and pop culture detailing made Cox's loafers super-funky and unashamedly full-on fun.

After churning out millions of pairs of loafers and swirling stilettos, Cox has now boldly applied the same principles to an exciting range of deliriously delicious cakes. A long-time fan of homemade sweets – his mother Maureen has been posting her delectable home-baked yummies to her beloved son in London from Canada for decades – he has now applied the same wit and irony to retail baking. Looking at a cupcake and cookie world festooned with gingham and butterflies, Cox decided to zig where others have zagged.

By commandeering a London Soho sex shop and teaming up with the baking genius of Eric Lanlard, who has made cakes for us for many years, Cox has virtually transformed the world of baked goods into an outrageously fun and delicious range of sinfully scrumptious madness.

Their Soho bake-shop has now become a must-see destination for the über-hip lover of indulgent sweeties, with a funky vibe. Opening a box of Cox Cookies & Cake cupcakes puts the biggest smile on your face and transports you to a place where the worries of the day melt away into delicious mouthfuls of sinful fun and outrageous fabulousness. We love the cakes almost as much as we love our Patsy!

SIR ELTON JOHN
& DAVID FURNISH

FOREWORD

I'm a designer. It's in my blood. It's who I am. It affects how I look at everything in the world. I see everyday objects, such as shoes, bags or cakes, and I want to make them sexier, inject them with glamour and make them shine! For me life is the triumph of the fantastic over the dull, and when I saw the pastel-shaded world of cupcakes, I wanted to shake it up, sex it up and create something breathtakingly new.

The result is Cox Cookies & Cake, a Soho bakery infused with seduction and style: The location in a former sex shop in the heart of London's historic red light district; the original Tracey Emin neon piece on the wall; the staff in leather-studded aprons; the mirrored ceilings and the polished black floor – all come together to set the scene for the most dangerous thing to hit the world of cupcakes since self-raising flour.

However, at the heart of what I do are the cakes themselves. Here I faced my limitations as a designer. I needed a skilled pâtissier and business partner to make sure the cakes tasted every bit as good as they looked, with all the quality that one associates with the Patrick Cox name. Fortunately Elizabeth Hurley introduced me to world-renowned and fabulous Eric Lanlard (he made Elizabeth's wedding cake) and as soon as we met I knew instantly we could work together and make the vision of Cox Cookies & Cake a reality.

Together we've created cakes that are sexy, unbelievably tasty and fun. They pay homage to sex, art, fashion and even politics. Each cake is like a work of art, yet unlike some of the shoes I used to make or Warhol paintings, our cakes are affordable and available for everyone.

This book takes that accessibility further. I want people to enjoy the design process themselves, have fun creating these cakes at home and see the same joy I see every day on the faces of my customers and in the reactions of their families and friends. So turn on the music, crank up the volume and get baking … Cox Cookies & Cake style!

PATRICK COX

Cox Cookies & Cake
13 Brewer Street, London W1F 0RH
11am–9pm Sunday to Thursday
11am–11pm Friday and Saturday
www.coxcookiesandcake.com

I'm a pâtissier. It's in my blood and who I am, or at least who I have been since I was a little boy staring in the windows of my local pâtisserie. In times where form often triumphs over substance and where looks too often succeed over taste, it has always been my mission to make cakes that taste as good as they look; cakes where the feasting of the eyes is not followed by a bite of disappointment, but by a feasting of the taste buds. I have been putting this philosophy into practice within my own business over the past 16 years, and with Cox Cookies & Cake I now have a new outlet for my naughtier skills.

Before having the pleasure of meeting Patrick, glamour was always very much part of my world, reflected in the title of my first book *Glamour Cakes* and my first two TV series' *Glamour Puds*. As an artisan I've always used cake design as my creative outlet. However, nothing had prepared me for the excitement I felt on first hearing about Patrick's vision, pushing my boundaries way beyond anything I would have dared to do myself.

The results of our efforts speak for themselves in the happy faces of our customers in the wonderful shop that Patrick has designed in the heart of Soho life. I hope this book enables you to bake a little of this excitement in your own home and put happy faces on your friends and family alike.

ERIC LANLARD

1

NUTTY & CHOCOLATEY CUPCAKES

FRUITY CUPCAKES

RICH & SPICY CUPCAKES

GUILT-FREE CUPCAKES

STYLING CUPCAKES

COOKIES

BARS & BISCUITS

miracles will delight kids and adults, too. The cola makes the cake light and airy, and the addition of the popping candy topping makes them a truly fun experience.

COLA CUPCAKES

MAKES 12 CUPCAKES

200g (7oz) unsalted butter
200ml (7fl oz) cola (I prefer to use
    the old-fashioned original one
    as it has more flavour)
250g (8oz) self-raising flour
1 tsp baking powder
1 tbsp cocoa powder
200g golden caster sugar
2 eggs, beaten
150ml (¼ pint) milk

FOR THE COLA FROSTING

100g (3½oz) unsalted butter,
    softened
25g (1oz) cocoa powder
450g (14½oz) icing sugar
100ml (3½fl oz) cola
1 tsp vanilla extract
cola-flavoured popping candy or
    fizzy cola bottles, to decorate

Preheat the oven to 200°C/fan 180°C/ gas mark 6, and line a cupcake tin with paper cases.

In a saucepan, gently heat the butter and cola until the butter has melted. Remove from the heat and leave to cool.

Sift the flour, baking powder and cocoa together. Add the cooled cola and butter mix, followed by the sugar, eggs and milk. Mix together until smooth.

Divide the mixture between the paper cases. Bake for 25–30 minutes, or until a skewer inserted into a cupcake comes out clean. Leave to cool in the tin for 5 minutes then transfer to a wire rack and allow to cool completely before frosting.

To make the Cola Frosting: cream the butter in a bowl. Sift the cocoa and icing sugar together and mix into the butter a little at a time, alternating with additions of the cola. Beat to give a nice smooth frosting. (You may need to add more cola if the frosting is too stiff). Beat in the vanilla extract.

Pipe the frosting on the cooled cupcakes and decorate with either popping candy or cola bottles.

This now celebrated cupcake is usually made as a large cake and there are many variations, including some that use beetroot juice to give the rich red colour. In this recipe I use a combination of pure cocoa, vinegar and red food colouring to achieve a vibrant tone.

RED VELVET CUPCAKES

MAKES 12 CUPCAKES

30g (1¼oz) cocoa powder
1 tsp vanilla extract
75g (3oz) unsalted butter, softened
175g (6oz) caster sugar
2 egg yolks
pinch of salt
150ml (¼ pint) buttermilk
150g (5oz) plain flour, sifted
½ tsp bicarbonate of soda
½ tsp white wine vinegar
1 tsp red food colouring

FOR THE FROSTING
125ml (4fl oz) milk
1½ tbsp flour
pinch of salt
100g (3½oz) unsalted butter, softened
175g (6oz) icing sugar, plus extra for dusting
100g (3½oz) white chocolate, melted and cooled
½ tsp vanilla extract

Preheat the oven to 200°C/fan 180°C/gas mark 6, and line a cupcake tin with paper cases.

In a small bowl, mix the cocoa and vanilla extract together and set aside.

In a large bowl, beat the butter and sugar together using a free-standing mixer or an electric hand whisk set on a medium-high speed. Add the egg yolks and beat for one more minute. Add the cocoa and vanilla to the mixture.

Stir the salt into the buttermilk, mix one-third into the mixture, followed by one-third of the flour. Repeat with two further batches of each until all are mixed in.

Mix the bicarbonate of soda with the vinegar and blend this and the food colouring into the batter. Divide the mixture between the paper cases and bake for 20–25 minutes, or until a skewer inserted into the centre of a cupcake comes out clean.

Allow the cupcakes to cool in the tin for 10 minutes. Then remove the cupcakes from the tin and allow to cool completely before frosting.

To make the frosting: in a small saucepan, whisk the milk, flour and salt over a medium heat for 1 or 2 minutes until the mixture thickens and begins to bubble. Transfer to a small bowl and leave to cool.

Beat the butter and icing sugar together until light and fluffy. Add the cooled chocolate, the milk mixture and the vanilla extract, and mix until smooth and fluffy.

Spread the frosting or pipe it on to the cooled cakes, and finish by crumbling some cooked red sponge on the top (you may have to sacrifice one of your cakes) and dust with icing sugar.

This is one for the chocoholics! There's cocoa, melted chocolate and chocolate chips in this beautiful moist cupcake. Then, for a rich finish, it's topped with chocolate frosting and chocolate sprinkles. Heaven!

TRIPLE CHOCOLATE CUPCAKES

MAKES 12 CUPCAKES

75g (3oz) dark chocolate, broken into pieces
200g (7oz) unsalted butter
225g (7½oz) caster sugar
3 eggs
½ tsp baking powder
175g (6oz) plain flour
25g (1oz) cocoa powder
50g (2oz) dark chocolate chips
1 quantity Chocolate Frosting (see page 91)
mixture of mini white, milk and dark chocolate sprinkles, to decorate

Preheat the oven to 200°C/fan 180°C/gas mark 6, and line a cupcake tin with paper cases.

In a large saucepan, melt the chocolate and butter over medium heat, stirring to prevent burning. Allow this to cool for a few minutes.

Stir in the sugar until well mixed. Add the eggs, one at a time, until you have a smooth batter. Sift the baking powder, flour and cocoa into the batter and mix until smooth. Fold in the chocolate chips.

Divide the mixture between the paper cases, but don't over-fill them, just about three-quarters full. Bake for 20–25 minutes, or until a skewer inserted into the centre of a cupcake comes out clean.

Leave to cool in the tins for 5 minutes then transfer to a wire rack and allow to cool completely before frosting. I like to top these with Chocolate Frosting and cover with mini chocolate sprinkles to decorate.

We call this classic the Irish cupcake because of the addition of Irish cream liqueur, which works perfectly with the chocolate base. Kids should be kept well away from these!

IRISH CREAM & CHOCOLATE CUPCAKES

MAKES 12 CUPCAKES

75g (3oz) dark chocolate, plus extra for decorating
200g (7oz) unsalted butter
225g (7½oz) caster sugar
1 tsp vanilla extract
1 tbsp of Irish cream liqueur
3 eggs
25g (1oz) cocoa powder
175g (6oz) plain flour
½ tsp baking powder
chocolate curls, to decorate

FOR THE FROSTING

225g (7½oz) unsalted butter
75g (3oz) dark chocolate, melted and cooled
550g (1lb 2oz) icing sugar
3 tbsp Irish cream liqueur

Preheat the oven to 200°C/fan 180°C/gas mark 6, and line a cupcake tin with paper cases.

Put the chocolate and butter together in a large heatproof bowl and place over a saucepan of barely simmering water, making sure the bowl does not touch the surface of the water. Stir until completely melted then remove from the heat. Stir in the sugar, vanilla extract and Irish cream liqueur.

Beat in the eggs one at a time. Sift in the cocoa powder, flour and baking powder and mix well until combined and smooth.

Spoon the mixture into the prepared cases, filling each three-quarters full. Bake for 20–25 minutes, or until a skewer inserted into the centre of a cupcake comes out clean.

Leave to cool in the tin for 5 minutes then transfer to a wire rack and allow to cool completely before covering with frosting.

To make the frosting: beat the butter into the melted chocolate until smooth. Gradually beat in the icing sugar and finally add the Irish cream liqueur. Using a small palette knife, spread the frosting over the cupcakes or pipe it on in spirals. Decorate with chocolate curls.

If you are a fan of the chocolate bar Bounty, these cupcakes are for you. Coated with a rich cinnamon ganache, they have a true taste of paradise.

CHOCOLATE & COCONUT CUPCAKES

MAKES 12 CUPCAKES

200g (7oz) caster sugar
200g (7oz) unsalted butter, softened
3 eggs
3 tbsp milk
175g (6oz) self-raising flour
½ tsp baking powder
75g (3oz) desiccated coconut

FOR THE CHOCOLATE GANACHE

150g (5oz) dark chocolate (55% cocoa solids), broken into small pieces
150ml (¼ pint) double cream
50g (2oz) very soft unsalted butter
1 tsp ground cinnamon
toasted desiccated coconut, to decorate

Preheat the oven to 200°C/fan 180°C/ gas mark 6, and line a cupcake tin with paper cases.

In a large bowl, cream the sugar and butter together until pale and fluffy using a free-standing mixer or electric hand whisk, then stir in the eggs one at a time, followed by the milk. Beat until everything is well incorporated.

Sift the flour and baking powder and fold them into butter mixture until smooth and well incorporated. Finally fold in the coconut.

Divide the mixture between the paper cases. Bake for 20 minutes or until a skewer inserted into a cupcake comes out clean. Leave to cool in the tin for 5 minutes and then transfer to a wire rack to cool completely.

To make the Chocolate Ganache: place the chocolate in a medium bowl. Put the cream in a small saucepan over a medium heat and, as soon as it reaches boiling point, pour it over the chocolate. Leave this to stand until the chocolate pieces have melted.

Once they are melted, pass the mixture through a sieve. Then stir in the softened butter and cinnamon, and leave to cool and slightly set.

Once the mixture has set use a free-standing mixer or an electric hand whisk, and beat until it has almost doubled in volume.

Spread the ganache over the cooled cupcakes and sprinkle with toasted desiccated coconut to decorate.

The rich dark chocolate cake and the sweetness of the raspberries is a combination made in heaven. Then, topped with chocolate frosting and more fresh raspberries… yum!

CHOCOLATE & RASPBERRY CUPCAKES

MAKES 12 CUPCAKES

125g (4oz) unsalted butter
75g (3oz) dark chocolate, broken into large pieces
1 tsp instant coffee
1 tsp vanilla essence
150g (5oz) light soft brown sugar
2 eggs, lightly beaten
1 tsp baking powder
225g (7½oz) self-raising flour
150ml (¼ pint) water
450g/14oz raspberries, plus extra to decorate
1 quantity Chocolate Frosting (see page 91)

Preheat the oven to 200°C/fan 180°C/gas mark 6, and line a cupcake tin with paper cases.

Melt the butter in a large heatproof bowl placed over a saucepan of barely simmering water, making sure the bowl does not touch the surface of the water. When it is half melted, add the chocolate. When the chocolate is completely melted remove from the heat and stir to mix in any lumps, then allow to cool for a few minutes.

Dissolve the coffee in the vanilla essence, then add this mixture and the brown sugar to the cooled chocolate and butter. When these are fully mixed together, add the eggs and mix in.

Sift the baking powder and the flour into the mixture and beat until all ingredients are well incorporated and the batter is thick. Then stir in the water a little at a time, making sure the liquid is entirely absorbed into the batter.

Divide the mixture between the paper cases, filling each about half full. Place 3 raspberries on the surface of each – they will sink into the batter. Then fill each case almost to the top and place another fresh raspberry on top.

Bake for about 25 minutes, or until each cupcake is firm to touch or a skewer inserted into a cupcake comes out clean. Leave to cool in the tin for 10 minutes and then transfer to a wire rack to cool completely. Once cool, pipe Chocolate Frosting in swirls on top of each cupcake and decorate with fresh raspberries on top.

Don't be put off by the lengthy preparation needed for this recipe – all the effort is well worth it to make these very tasty grown-up cakes. I like using Amarena cherries if I can get them – Italian delis often stock them.

BLACK FOREST CUPCAKES

MAKES 12 CUPCAKES

425g (14oz) jar or can of stoned cherries in syrup, drained (reserving the syrup)
100g (3½oz) dark chocolate (50% cocoa solids), broken into pieces
165g (5½oz) unsalted butter, roughly chopped
300g (10oz) caster sugar
4 tbsp cherry brandy
150g (5oz) plain flour, sifted
2 tbsp self-raising flour, sifted
2 tbsp cocoa powder
1 egg

FOR THE DECORATION
2 tsp cherry brandy
200ml (7fl oz) whipping cream
50g (2oz) chunk of dark chocolate (50% cocoa solids, optional)

Preheat the oven to 200°C/fan 180°C/gas mark 6, and line a cupcake tin with paper cases.

Put 100g (3½oz) of the cherries and 125ml (4fl oz) of their syrup in a food processor and process until it becomes a smooth purée.

Cut the remaining cherries in half and reserve the rest of the syrup.

Place the cherry purée in a saucepan together with the chocolate, butter, sugar and cherry brandy. Stir over a low heat until the chocolate has melted. Pour into a large bowl and allow to cool for 15 minutes.

When cool, whisk in the flours and the cocoa powder, followed by the egg. It will be very runny, but that is OK.

Divide the mixture between the paper cases. You will probably find that you fill the cases close to the top, but do not worry, as the cupcakes will not rise a great deal.

Bake for 40–45 minutes, or until firm to touch or until a skewer inserted into a cupcake comes out clean. Allow to cool in the tin for 5 minutes then transfer to a wire rack to cool completely.

To decorate, mix the cherry brandy into the remaining cherry halves. Whip the cream to soft peaks, and pipe swirls on top of each cake.

Top each cake with some of the brandy-soaked cherry halves and drizzle over the reserved syrup. If using, scrape along the side of the chocolate with a vegetable peeler to create curls and use these to decorate the top of each cake.

For this recipe I use a mixture of mini marshmallows and Marshmallow Fluff to top a rich and gooey brownie-like cupcake. If you haven't used Marshmallow Fluff before, seek it out from specialist food halls and American food stores – it gives these little devilish cupcakes a fun, toasted-marshmallow dimension and an extra marshmallow hit!

CHOCOLATE & MARSHMALLOW CUPCAKES

MAKES 12 CUPCAKES

75g (3oz) dark chocolate, broken into pieces
200g (7oz) unsalted butter
225g (7½oz) caster sugar
3 eggs
½ tsp baking powder
25g (1oz) cocoa powder
175g (6oz) plain flour
icing sugar, to decorate

FOR THE MARSHMALLOW BUTTERCREAM FROSTING
250g (8oz) unsalted butter, softened
125g (4oz) Marshmallow Fluff, plus extra to decorate
mini marshmallows, to decorate (optional)

Preheat the oven to 200°C/fan 180°C/gas mark 6, and line a cupcake tin with paper cases.

In a large saucepan over medium heat, melt the chocolate and butter, stirring to prevent any burning. Allow to cool for a few minutes, then stir in sugar until well mixed.

Add the eggs, one at a time, until you have a smooth batter. Then sift in the baking powder, flour and cocoa and mix just until smooth.

Divide the mixture between the paper cases filling them about three-quarters full – don't over fill them. Bake for 20–25 minutes or until a skewer inserted into a cupcake comes out clean. Leave to cool in the tin for 10 minutes and then transfer to a wire rack to cool completely.

To make the Marshmallow Buttercream Frosting: beat the butter and Marshmallow Fluff together until smooth. Using a small palette knife, spread the frosting on top of the cupcakes. If you want to add an extra marshmallow hit, spoon a couple of teaspoons of Fluff on top of the frosting, add some mini marshmallows, if liked, and dust with icing sugar.

Beware! The Fluff will drip down the frosting, so don't let these cakes hang around for too long – although I love the way they look when this happens.

What makes this banana cupcake special is the roasting of the banana – its flavour becomes much more intense and sweet. You can decorate these with a classic Vanilla Buttercream Frosting, but I like eating them while still warm served with vanilla ice cream.

BANANA WALNUT CUPCAKES

MAKES 12 CUPCAKES

3 soft medium-sized bananas, peeled and sliced
100g (3½oz) soft dark brown sugar
1 tsp grated nutmeg
150g (5oz) unsalted butter, softened
150g (5oz) soft brown sugar
4 eggs, lightly beaten
150g (5oz) self-raising wholemeal flour
½ tsp baking powder
1 quantity Vanilla Buttercream Frosting (see page 88)
75g (3oz) walnuts, roughly chopped, plus extra to decorate (optional)

Preheat the oven to 200°C/fan 180°C/gas mark 6, and line a cupcake tin with paper cases.

Place the walnuts on a baking tray and toast in the oven for 5 minutes, making sure they do not burn.

Place the banana slices on a large piece of foil and sprinkle with the dark brown sugar, then sprinkle over the nutmeg. Wrap the foil around the banana mixture and bake for 20–25 minutes, or until soft and mushy. Set aside to cool.

In a large bowl, cream the butter and soft brown sugar until light and fluffy, then gradually beat in the eggs. Sift the flour and baking powder and fold them into the mixture.

Once the bananas have cooled, place a sieve over a bowl and put the banana mixture carefully into the sieve. Allow the sugary liquid to drain into the bowl and discard. Tip the banana pieces into a clean bowl and mash them, then fold them and the walnuts into the mixture.

Divide the mixture between the paper cases and bake for 20–25 minutes, or until a skewer inserted into the centre of a cupcake comes out clean.

These are great served warm with ice cream or alternatively spread with Vanilla Buttercream Frosting and top with some chopped walnuts, if liked.

This recipe uses a very soft coconut sponge with an indulgent mascarpone icing. I like using long strands of dry coconut for the topping. To spoil yourself, try drizzling a bit of melted dark chocolate on top. This recipe can be made very grown-up by the addition of some Malibu coconut liqueur!

COCONUT CUPCAKES

MAKES 12 CUPCAKES

175g (6oz) unsalted butter, softened
125g (4oz) caster sugar
3 eggs, beaten
20g (¾oz) cocoa powder
50g (2oz) desiccated coconut
150g (5oz) plain flour
1 tsp baking powder
4 tbsp milk

FOR THE FROSTING

300g (10oz) mascarpone
50g (2oz) icing sugar
zest of 1 lime
50g (2oz) desiccated coconut
40g (1½oz) thin strands of fresh
    coconut, toasted

Preheat the oven to 200°C/fan 180°C/gas mark 6, and line a cupcake tin with paper cases.

In a large bowl, cream together the butter and sugar until pale and light. Add the beaten eggs and mix well. Add the cocoa powder and coconut, and mix in well. Mix together the flour, baking powder and then fold into the butter-and-egg mixture. Add the milk and mix until smooth.

Divide the mixture between the paper cases and bake on the middle shelf of the oven for 20 minutes, or until the cakes are golden and a skewer inserted into the centre of a cupcake comes out clean. Leave to cool in the tin for 5 minutes and then transfer to a wire rack to cool completely.

To make the frosting: mix the mascarpone, icing sugar and lime zest together until smooth. Add the desiccated coconut and mix in well. When ready, spread an even layer of the mascarpone mixture over the top of each cake and sprinkle with toasted coconut.

Here are all the Middle Eastern flavours in a cute little cupcake – the combination of the spices, floral essences and nuts works so well. I like to top mine with dried organic rose petals.

PISTACHIO & ROSEWATER CUPCAKES

MAKES 12 CUPCAKES

125ml (4fl oz) natural yoghurt
160ml (5½fl oz) milk
5 tbsp sunflower oil
175g (6oz) caster sugar
1½ tbsp rosewater
175g (6oz) plain flour
2 tbsp cornflour
½ tsp bicarbonate of soda
½ tsp baking powder
1 tsp vanilla extract
generous pinch of cardamom
    seeds (the little black seeds
    inside cardamom pods)
50g (2oz) chopped pistachios

FOR THE ROSEWATER GLAZE
200g (7oz) icing sugar
15g (½oz) unsalted butter
2–3 tsp milk
½ tsp rosewater

Preheat the oven to 200°C/fan 180°C/gas mark 6, and line a cupcake tin with paper cases.

In a large bowl, whisk together the yoghurt, milk, oil, sugar and rosewater. Sift in the flour, cornflour, bicarbonate of soda and baking powder, then stir in the vanilla extract, cardamom seeds and chopped pistachios.

Divide the mixture between the paper cases, but only fill them three-quarters full. Bake for 20–25 minutes, or until a skewer inserted into the centre of a cupcake comes out clean.

Leave to cool in the tin for 5 minutes and then transfer to a wire rack to cool completely before covering with the rosewater glaze.

To make the Rosewater Glaze: cream together half the icing sugar and all the butter until the mixture resembles fine crumbs, then mix in the milk and rosewater. Finally beat in the remaining icing sugar. Spread the glaze on top of the cupcakes to finish.

These little marvels are so moreish, with a pistachio sponge topped with Italian meringue and nutty praline. They also look very pretty, with the praline shining like jewels.

PISTACHIO & PRALINE CUPCAKES

MAKES 12 CUPCAKES

125g (4fl oz) unsalted butter, softened
175g (6oz) caster sugar
seeds from ½ vanilla pod
75g (3oz) pistachio paste
2 eggs
185g (6½oz) plain flour
1 tsp baking powder
125ml (4fl oz) milk

FOR THE PISTACHIO PRALINE
sunflower oil, for brushing
75g (3oz) unsalted pistachio nuts
200g (7oz) caster sugar
125ml (4fl oz) water

FOR THE MERINGUE TOPPING
150g (5oz) caster sugar
3 tbsp water
generous pinch of cream of tartar
2 egg whites
pinch of salt

Preheat the oven to 200°C/fan 180°C/gas mark 6, and line a cupcake tin with paper cases.

Beat together the butter, sugar, vanilla seeds and pistachio paste until light and creamy. Gradually add the eggs and beat again. Sift in the flour and baking powder, and beat until combined. Add the milk and mix in. Divide the mixture between the paper cases. Bake for 15–17 minutes, or until a skewer inserted into the centre of a cupcake comes out clean. Remove from the tin and transfer to a wire rack to cool.

To make the Pistachio Praline: line a baking sheet with foil, brush it with sunflower oil and scatter the nuts on top. Place the sugar and water in a saucepan over a low heat, stirring until the sugar has dissolved. Increase the heat and bring to the boil, brushing any sugar crystals down the inside of the pan with a wet pastry brush. Cook for 8–10 minutes or until dark golden. Remove from the heat and pour over the nuts. Leave to cool, then chop into small chunks.

To make the Meringue Topping: combine the sugar, water and cream of tartar in a heavy-based saucepan, and stir over a medium heat until it boils. Using a sugar thermometer, when the syrup reaches 110°C (230°F), whisk the egg whites, ideally in a free-standing mixer, until stiff. When the syrup reaches 120°C (250°F), with the mixer still on, slowly pour the syrup into the egg whites down the side of the bowl avoiding the whisk. Beat until the meringue is thick, glossy and completely cold, about 10–15 minutes. To decorate, pipe the meringue over the cupcakes (see page 98 for styling tips). Arrange a few nuggets of pistachio praline on top.

This all-American classic is such a versatile recipe: usually made as a loaf, a round, or baked in a tin as a tray-bake – but now as cupcakes! In a lot of their recipes, our US cousins use oil as a fat which gives you a very moist cake. The cream cheese frosting is rich and delicious, but do make sure you use a very dry cream cheese to give you a nice firm texture. These cakes will keep very well in a tin, but do not store them in the fridge, as they will go hard.

CARROT CAKE CUPCAKES

MAKES 12 CUPCAKES

250ml (8fl oz) sunflower or corn oil
225g (7½oz) golden caster sugar
3 eggs
225g (7½oz) self-raising flour
1 tsp ground cinnamon
1 tsp ground nutmeg
250g (8oz) carrots, coarsely grated
100g (3½oz) sultanas, plus extra
   to decorate
100g (3½oz) chopped walnuts,
   plus extra to decorate

FOR THE CREAM CHEESE FROSTING

200g (7oz) half-fat cream cheese
100g (3½oz) unrefined golden
   icing sugar, sifted
finely grated zest of 1 orange

Preheat the oven to 200°C/fan 180°C/ gas mark 6, and line a cupcake tin with paper cases.

Pour the oil into a large bowl, add the caster sugar and mix with a large whisk for a few minutes, then add the eggs one at a time.

Sift the flour, cinnamon and nutmeg, and using a large metal spoon, fold the flour into the egg mix. Fold the carrots, sultanas and walnuts into the mixture.

Divide the mixture between the paper cases and bake for 20 minutes, or until a skewer inserted into the centre of a cupcake comes out clean. Leave to cool in the tin for 5 minutes and then transfer to a wire rack to cool completely.

To make the Cream Cheese Frosting: gently mix the cream cheese until soft and smooth, and then gradually add the icing sugar, followed by the orange zest.

When the cakes are cold, use a small palette knife to spread the frosting on the top of each cake and decorate with few sultanas and walnuts.

These cupcakes are just so delicious; the combination of the rich chocolate and the salty crunchy peanut butter work wonderfully.

CHOCOLATE PEANUT BUTTER CUPCAKES

MAKES 12 CUPCAKES

175g (6oz) unsalted butter
150g (5oz) caster sugar
150g (5oz) light brown sugar
2 eggs
2 tsp vanilla extract
240ml (7¾fl oz) buttermilk
125ml (4fl oz) sour cream
2 tbsp espresso coffee
2 tbsp crunchy peanut butter
250g (8oz) plain flour
100g (3½oz) cocoa powder
1½ tsp baking powder

FOR THE PEANUT BUTTER FROSTING

150g (5oz) icing sugar
110g (3¾oz) smooth peanut butter
50g (2oz) unsalted butter, softened
¾ tsp vanilla extract
2 tbsp double cream
chopped salted peanuts, to
    decorate

Preheat the oven to 200°C/fan 180°C/gas mark 6, and line a cupcake tin with paper cases.

Cream the butter with both sugars, ideally in the bowl of a free-standing mixer or using an electric hand whisk, on high speed until light and fluffy – about 5 minutes. Lower the speed to medium, and add the eggs one at a time. Then add the vanilla extract and mix in well.

In another bowl, whisk together the buttermilk, sour cream, coffee and peanut butter.

Into a third bowl, sift together the flour, cocoa and baking powder.

On low speed add one-third of the buttermilk mixture followed by one-third of the flour, mix only until just blended. Repeat until all the buttermilk and flour are incorporated. Fold the batter with a spatula to be sure it is completely blended. Divide the batter between the cupcake cases. Bake for 20–25 minutes, or until a skewer inserted into the centre of a cupcake comes out clean. Leave to cool in the tin for 5 minutes, then transfer to a wire rack to cool completely.

To make the Peanut Butter Frosting: mix the icing sugar, peanut butter, butter and vanilla extract in a free-standing mixer on a medium-low speed until creamy, scraping down the bowl with a spatula as you work – alternatively use an electric hand whisk. Add the cream and beat on high speed until the mixture is light and smooth. Using a piping bag with a small round nozzle, pipe the frosting onto each cupcake (see page 98 for styling tips) and finish with a sprinkling of chopped salted peanuts.

2

These fresh, zesty cupcakes make great summer treats. You could add some chopped fresh mint to turn them into Mojito cupcakes, and a cup of roasted coconut in the mix works very well, too. Its a good idea to make the crystallized lime peel decoration the day before you want to serve these cakes.

KEY LIME CUPCAKES

MAKES 12 CUPCAKES

175g (6oz) unsalted butter, softened
300g (10oz) caster sugar
3 eggs
finely grated zest of 1 lime and
    4 tbsp juice
1 tsp vanilla extract
300g (10oz) plain flour
1 tsp baking powder
360ml (12½fl oz) buttermilk

FOR THE CRYSTALLIZED LIME PEEL

2 unwaxed limes
100g (3½oz) caster sugar, plus
    extra to coat
100ml (3½fl oz) water

FOR THE LIME SYRUP

30g (1¼oz) icing sugar dissolved
    in the juice of 1½ limes

FOR THE WHITE CHOCOLATE FROSTING

200g (7oz) white chocolate, broken
    into pieces
125ml (4fl oz) whipping cream
175g (6oz) unsalted butter, softened
grated zest of 1 lime and juice of ½
350g (11½oz) icing sugar

To make the Crystallized Lime Peel: pare the peel from each lime, then carefully cut it into thin strips. Put the caster sugar and the water in a pan and bring to the boil, stirring. Once bubbling, add one-third of the lime peel and cook for 3–4 minutes. Remove the peel, roll gently in caster sugar and lay them on greaseproof paper. (Don't arrange them on top of each other or they will stick together.) Repeat with the remaining peel and leave to dry overnight.

Preheat the oven to 200°C/fan 180°C/gas mark 6, and line a cupcake tin with paper cases.

Using a free-standing mixer or electric hand whisk, cream the butter and sugar until pale and fluffy. Add the eggs, slowly, one at the time. Then add the lime zest and juice, and the vanilla extract. In another bowl, sift together the flour and baking powder. Gradually add this to the butter mixture with alternate spoonfuls of buttermilk. Divide the mixture between the paper cases and bake for 25–30 minutes, or until a skewer inserted into the centre of a cupcake comes out clean. Leave to cool in the tins for 5 minutes then transfer to a wire rack. Whilst warm, use a cocktail stick to insert small holes all over each cupcake, spoon over a teaspoon of lime syrup and allow it to soak and cool before frosting.

To make the frosting: melt the chocolate with the cream in a heatproof bowl over a saucepan of simmering water, making sure the bowl does not touch the surface of the water. Allow to cool completely. Then whisk in the butter, lime zest, juice and icing sugar. When smooth, use a piping bag to pipe the frosting onto each cake, and decorate with a few strands of crystallized lime peel.

This light and zesty sponge carries off the rich white chocolate frosting with serious style, making a great summer dessert.

ZESTY LEMON & WHITE CHOCOLATE CUPCAKES

MAKES 12 CUPCAKES

160g (5½oz) unsalted butter, softened
100g (3½oz) caster sugar
2 eggs
200ml (7fl oz) natural yoghurt
grated zest of 1 lemon and 2 tsp lemon juice
½ tsp lemon oil
200g (7oz) plain flour
1 tsp baking powder
2 tsp poppy seeds
½ a 320g jar of lemon curd

FOR THE WHITE CHOCOLATE FROSTING

75g (3oz) unsalted butter
75g (3oz) cream cheese
150g (5oz) icing sugar
100g (3½oz) white chocolate, melted, plus extra to decorate

Preheat the oven to 200°C/fan 180°C/gas mark 6, and line a cupcake tin with paper cases.

In a large bowl, cream the butter and sugar together until light and fluffy. Then mix in the eggs, one at a time, followed by the yoghurt, lemon zest and juice and the lemon oil. Sift the flour and baking powder together and stir this into the butter mixture with the poppy seeds until just combined.

Divide the mixture between the paper cases, just filling them half-full. Spoon some lemon curd over each and then top to the rim with the remaining batter. Bake for about 25–30 minutes, or until a skewer inserted into the side of a cupcake comes out clean. Leave to cool in the tins for 5 minutes then transfer to a wire rack and allow to cool completely before frosting.

To make the White Chocolate Frosting: cream together the butter, cream cheese and icing sugar, then add the melted white chocolate. Either spread the frosting using a small palette knife or pipe the frosting over the cooled cupcakes. Sprinkle with white chocolate curls and leave to set.

This could almost be a breakfast cupcake!
When I can get hold of it I make mine with blood
orange marmalade and a homemade version
make these cupcakes even more divine.

ORANGE MARMALADE CUPCAKES

MAKES 12 CUPCAKES

150g (5oz) unsalted butter, softened
100g (3½oz) golden caster sugar
2 eggs
finely grated zest of 2 oranges and
    2 tbsp juice
3 tbsp Seville orange marmalade,
    plus extra to decorate
1 tsp vanilla extract
250g (8oz) self-raising flour

FOR THE FROSTING
1 quantity Vanilla Buttercream
    Frosting (see page 88)
finely grated zest of 1 orange

Preheat the oven to 200°C/fan 180°C/
gas mark 6, and line a cupcake tin with
paper cases.

In a large bowl, cream together the
butter and sugar. Add the eggs one at
a time. Mix in the orange zest and juice,
the marmalade and vanilla extract. Sift
the flour into the mixture and combine
until smooth.

Divide the mixture between the paper
cupcake cases and bake for about
20–25 minutes, until a skewer inserted
into the centre of a cupcake comes out
clean. Leave to cool in the tin for
5 minutes and then transfer to a wire
rack and allow to cool completely
before frosting.

Decorate the cupcakes with Vanilla
Buttercream Frosting mixed with the
orange zest, and top each cupcake
with a teaspoon of marmalade.

This is a nice autumn recipe, perfect for Halloween celebrations. You can find tins of cooked pumpkin in specialist food stores, especially those that have American foods sections.

ORANGE & PUMPKIN CUPCAKES

MAKES 12 CUPCAKES

300g (10oz) plain flour
1 tbsp baking powder
½ tsp bicarbonate of soda
½ tsp ground ginger
¾ tsp ground cinnamon
½ tsp ground nutmeg
grated zest of 1 orange
100g (3½oz) unsalted butter, softened
200g (7oz) caster sugar
2 eggs
225g (7½oz) cooked and mashed or canned pumpkin
175ml (6fl oz) milk

FOR THE MASCARPONE FROSTING

300g (10oz) mascarpone cheese
75g (3oz) icing sugar, sifted
grated zest of 1 orange and
    1 tbsp juice

Preheat the oven to 200°C/fan 180°C/gas mark 6, and line a cupcake tin with paper cases.

In a large bowl, sift together the flour, baking powder, bicarbonate of soda, ginger, cinnamon and nutmeg, then stir in the grated orange zest.

In another bowl, cream together the butter and sugar until light and fluffy. Then beat in the eggs, one at a time. Blend the pumpkin into this mixture and then stir in the sifted dry ingredients, a little at a time, alternating with some of the milk, blending after each addition, until the batter is smooth.

Divide the mixture between the paper cases and bake for 25 minutes, or until a skewer inserted into the centre of a cupcake comes out clean. Leave to cool in the tin for 5 minutes then transfer to a wire rack and allow to cool completely before frosting.

To make the Mascarpone Frosting: beat the mascarpone cheese until light and smooth, and then gradually add the icing sugar, stirring after each addition. Stir in the grated orange zest and juice, and mix until smooth. Using a small palette knife, spread the frosting over each cake.

The classic lemon meringue pie turned into a delicious cupcake… why not serve these as a dessert and add a few berries for an extra finishing touch.

LEMON MERINGUE CUPCAKES

MAKES 12 CUPCAKES

100g (3½oz) unsalted butter, softened
100g (3½oz) caster sugar
seeds from 1 vanilla pod
2 eggs
100g (3½oz) self-raising flour, sifted
finely grated zest of 1 lemon, plus a few strips to decorate
75g (3oz) lemon curd

FOR THE MERINGUE
2 egg whites
100g (3½oz) caster sugar

Preheat the oven to 200°C/fan 180°C/gas mark 6, and line a cupcake tin with paper cases.

In a large mixing bowl, ideally using an electric hand whisk, cream together the butter, sugar and vanilla seeds until the mixture is pale, fluffy and well combined. Crack in the eggs one at a time, and beat in until both are fully incorporated into the mixture. Fold in the sifted flour and the lemon zest until well combined.

Divide the mixture between the paper cases and add a teaspoonful of lemon curd to the top of each cupcake. Bake for 15–20 minutes, or until they are pale golden-brown and spring back when pressed lightly in the centre.

While the cupcakes are baking, make the meringue: whisk the egg whites until they form soft peaks. Gradually add the sugar, whisking continuously, until stiff peaks form again. The mixture should be thick and glossy.

When the cakes have cooked, turn off the oven and preheat the grill to its highest setting.

Spoon the meringue into a piping bag with a small plain nozzle and pipe it on top of each cupcake. To create a spikey effect, pipe small dots in a circle around the rim, pushing the bag down and up sharply to make a point, then repeat in a spiral until you reach the centre.

Place the cupcakes under a hot grill for 2 minutes to colour the meringue (or you can use a kitchen blow-torch).

The great British tradition of strawberries and cream in a cheeky cupcake. These are perfect for an al fresco lunch or picnic.

STRAWBERRY & CREAM CUPCAKES

MAKES 12 CUPCAKES

175g (6oz) unsalted butter, softened
175g (6oz) caster sugar
3 eggs, beaten
1 tsp vanilla extract
175g (6oz) self-raising flour, sifted

FOR THE FROSTING
175g (6oz) strawberries, plus 6 extra
    to decorate
300g (10oz) full-fat cream cheese
225g (7½oz) icing sugar, sifted

Preheat the oven to 200°C/fan 180°C/gas mark 6, and line a cupcake tin with paper cases.

Cream the butter and sugar together until light and fluffy, then gradually beat in the eggs. When the eggs have been incorporated add the vanilla extract and fold in the flour.

Divide the mixture between the paper cases and bake for about 20 minutes, or until they have risen and are golden. Leave to cool in the tins for 5 minutes then transfer to a wire rack and allow to cool completely before frosting.

To make the frosting: blend or mash the strawberries to a purée, then pass through a fine-meshed sieve to remove the seeds. Beat the cream cheese, icing sugar and strawberry purée together to form a smooth and shiny icing. Transfer to a piping bag and pipe the frosting on to the cooled cakes (see page 98 for piping tips), then top each cupcake with half a strawberry.

We sell loads of these delicious blueberry compote 'Kiss cakes' at Cox Cookies & Cake. I like to add the berries in the centre in order to enhance the flavour and provide a nice surprise when cutting or biting into the cupcake. In the shop we decorate them with chocolate lips painted with red edible colouring, but you can top yours with whatever you like.

BLUEBERRY COMPOTE CUPCAKES

MAKES 12 CUPCAKES

2 eggs
200g (7oz) caster sugar
125ml (4fl oz) sunflower oil
¼ tsp vanilla extract
250g (8oz) plain flour
pinch of salt
½ tsp baking powder
250ml (8fl oz) soured cream
1 quantity Vanilla Buttercream
    Frosting (see page 88)

FOR THE BLUEBERRY COMPOTE
150g (5oz) blueberries
50g (2oz) caster sugar

First make the Blueberry Compote: place the blueberries and the sugar in a small saucepan over a low heat and cook gently until the fruits start to pop, stirring to prevent the sugar from catching. Leave to cool. If your compote has produced a lot of liquid, strain a little into a bowl so not to add too much extra liquid to your cakes (this spare juice will come in handy later!).

Preheat the oven to 200°C/fan 180°C/gas mark 6, and line a cupcake tin with paper cases.

In a large bowl, beat the eggs, gradually adding the sugar while beating. Continue beating and slowly pour in the oil. Stir in the vanilla extract. In a separate bowl sift together the flour, salt and baking powder. Stir these dry ingredients into the egg mixture in small amounts alternating with the soured cream.

Spoon some of the mixture into the paper cases just to fill them half full, then spoon 1½ teaspoons of the compote on top. Top each with another spoonful of batter to cover and fill almost to the top of the case.

Cook for 25 minutes, or until a skewer inserted into the side of a cupcake comes out clean. Leave to cool in the tins for 5 minutes then transfer to a wire rack and allow to cool completely before frosting.

Pipe Vanilla Buttercream Frosting in spirals on top of each cupcake and spoon over any excess compote you have remaining and some of the lovely blueberry juice.

For this recipe you must get the beautiful stalks of red/pink 'champagne' rhubarb that are in season at the beginning of the year. As well as being less fibrous, this gives a lovely colour to these cute cupcakes.

RHUBARB CUPCAKES

MAKES 12 CUPCAKES

250g (8oz) unsalted butter, softened
175g (6oz) soft brown sugar
3 eggs
225g (7½oz) self-raising flour
2 tsp ground ginger
175ml (6fl oz) milk
1 quantity Vanilla Buttercream
    Frosting (see page 88)

FOR THE BAKED RHUBARB STRIPS

2 stalks of pink rhubarb
icing sugar, for dusting

FOR THE RHUBARB COMPOTE

125g (4oz) rhubarb, trimmed and
    cut into small dice
30g (1¼oz) caster sugar
1 tsp ground ginger
1 tbsp water

It is best to make the baked rhubarb strips the day before: preheat the oven to 120°C/fan 100°C/gas mark ½. With a very sharp knife, cut the rhubarb stalks into 10cm (4-inch) pieces and then cut very thin lengths from each piece. Place on a baking tray lined with baking paper or a silicone mat, dust icing sugar over the top and bake for 2–3 hours, or until dried out and crisp. Be careful not to overcook or you will lose the beautiful pink shade.

Preheat the oven to 200°C/fan 180°C/ gas mark 6, and line a cupcake tin with paper cases.

Cream the butter and sugar until pale and fluffy. Add the eggs and then slowly add the milk. Sift in the flour and ginger. Divide the mixture between the paper cases and bake for 18–20 minutes, or until a skewer inserted into the centre of a cupcake comes out clean. Leave to cool in the tin for 5 minutes then transfer to a wire rack and allow to cool completely.

To make the Rhubarb Compote: place all the ingredients in a small pan and heat gently to boiling point (you just want the rhubarb to release its natural juices and turn a beautiful shade of pink). Leave to bubble and reduce for 2–3 minutes. Once the rhubarb has softened and the liquid has gone syrupy, remove from the heat and leave to cool completely.

Use a 2cm- (¾ inch-) wide cutter to cut 1cm (⅓ inch) deep into the centre of each cupcake to leave a space for the compote. Spoon the compote into these spaces and then pipe vanilla frosting over the top. Once the frosting has set, arrange the dried pieces of baked rhubarb decoratively on top of each cupcake.

With their crumbly topping, these are more of a dessert than a cupcake – you could even serve them hot with runny custard.

APPLE CRUMBLE CUPCAKES

MAKES 12 CUPCAKES

2 cooking apples, peeled, cored
    and chopped
1 tsp ground cinnamon
½ tsp bicarbonate of soda
100g (3½oz) butter, softened
200g (7oz) soft brown sugar
2 eggs
350g (11½oz) self-raising flour
icing sugar, for dusting

FOR THE CRUMBLE TOPPING
50g (2oz) plain flour
50g (2oz) soft brown sugar
½ tsp ground cinnamon
40g (1½oz) cold unsalted butter

Preheat the oven to 200°C/fan 180°C/ gas mark 6, and line a cupcake tin with paper cases.

First make the crumble topping; put the flour, sugar and cinnamon in a bowl. With your fingertips, rub the unsalted butter into the flour mix until the mixture resembles breadcrumbs. Set this mixture to one side.

Put the apples in a saucepan with the cinnamon and cook over a gentle heat until mushy. Leave to cool, then drain through a fine-meshed sieve to remove any liquid, then weigh out 250g (8oz) of the apple.

In a bowl, mix the bicarbonate of soda into the apples. In a large bowl, cream the butter and sugar together, and then add the eggs. Fold the self-raising flour and the apples alternately into the butter mixture and mix well.

Divide the mixture between the paper cases. Sprinkle the crumble mix over the tops and bake for 20–25 minutes, or until golden brown on top and a skewer inserted into the centre of a cupcake comes out clean.

Leave to cool in the tins for 5 minutes then transfer to a wire rack and allow to cool completely. When cool, finish with a dusting of icing sugar.

This recipe is inspired by a fabulous dessert of spit-roasted baby pineapple with Amaretto that I once had in Mauritius… all the flavours are here in these cupcakes.

MAURITIUS PINEAPPLE CUPCAKES

MAKES 12 CUPCAKES

175g (6oz) plain flour
30g (1¼oz) ground almonds
1 tsp baking powder
125g (4oz) unsalted butter, softened
300g (10oz) golden caster sugar
3 eggs at room temperature
1 tsp pure vanilla extract
½ tsp pure almond extract
125ml (4fl oz) milk
90ml (3fl oz) Amaretto
400ml (14fl oz) double cream

FOR THE FLAMBÉED PINEAPPLE

100g (3½oz) caster sugar
1 small pineapple, peeled, cored
    and cut into small dice
100ml (3½fl oz) Amaretto
100ml (3½fl oz) double cream
1 tbsp fresh orange juice
seeds from 1 vanilla pod

Preheat the oven to 200°C/fan 180°C/gas mark 6, and line a cupcake tin with paper cases.

In a bowl, mix together the flour, ground almonds and baking powder. In another large bowl, cream the butter and sugar until pale and fluffy. Add the eggs, one at a time, beating until each is incorporated. Mix in the vanilla and almond extracts. Add the flour mixture in three batches, alternating with the milk in two additions, and mixing until just combined. If using an electric hand whisk, reduce the speed to low.

Divide the mixture between the paper cases, to fill each three-quarters full. Bake for 18–20 minutes, or until a skewer inserted into the centre of a cupcake comes out clean. Set the tin on a wire rack and immediately poke little holes over the tops of the cupcakes with a cocktail stick then pour a teaspoon of Amaretto over the tops. Allow to cool completely before removing from the tin.

To make the Flambéed Pineapple: in a large pan, heat the sugar over a medium heat, stirring, until the sugar dissolves and turns golden brown. Add the chopped pineapple and carefully toss it in the dissolved sugar. Carefully pour in the Amaretto and ignite the alcohol. Once the flames subside and the caramel melts, if there is a lot of liquid in the pan at this stage strain a little away. Then stir in the cream, orange juice and vanilla seeds. Boil, stirring occasionally, until thickened, for about 5 minutes. Remove from the heat and allow to cool completely. When ready to serve, whip the cream to soft peaks and spread over the top of each cooled cupcake. Top with a generous spoonful of Flambéed Pineapple.

3

The rich chocolate and all the lovely exotic spices in these cakes work very well together, and just when you thought you'd tasted everything, a lovely hot sensation hits you as the cayenne chilli-flavoured frosting works its wonders… another one for adults only!

MEXICAN CHOCOLATE CUPCAKES

MAKES 12 CUPCAKES

175g (6oz) plain flour
225g (7½oz) caster sugar
4 tbsp cocoa powder
1 tsp bicarbonate of soda
1 tsp cinnamon
¼ tsp ground nutmeg
1 tsp vanilla extract
1 tbsp white wine vinegar
5 tbsp sunflower oil
chilli pepper cake decorations,
    to decorate

FOR THE FROSTING

100g (3½oz) dark chocolate,
    broken into pieces
150g (5oz) unsalted butter
150g (5oz) icing sugar
¼ tsp ground cayenne pepper

Preheat the oven to 200°C/fan 180°C/gas mark 6, and line a cupcake tin with paper cases.

Sift together the flour, sugar, cocoa, bicarbonate of soda, cinnamon and nutmeg into a bowl. In a large bowl, blend together the vanilla extract, vinegar, oil and 250ml (8fl oz) cold water. Mix the dry ingredients into this mixture until well combined and the batter is smooth – a free-standing mixer or an electric hand whisk will help in doing this.

Divide the mixture between the paper cases (it will be fairly liquid, so you may want to use a jug) and bake for 20–25 minutes, or until a skewer inserted into the centre of a cupcake comes out clean. Allow to cool in the tin for 5 minutes, and then transfer to a wire rack to cool completely.

To make the frosting: melt the chocolate in a heatproof bowl placed over a saucepan of barely simmering water, making sure the bowl does not touch the surface of the water. When melted leave to cool.

Whisk the butter and icing sugar together until pale and fluffy, then whisk in the cooled melted chocolate and the cayenne pepper. Pipe the frosting onto the cooled cakes and top with chilli pepper cake decorations to finish.

This is my favourite Italian dessert in a cupcake. The light coffee sponge topped with a mascarpone and Marsala frosting makes a quite delicious combination. These cupcakes must be eaten on the day they are made.

TIRAMISU CUPCAKES

MAKES 12 CUPCAKES

50g (2oz) unsalted butter
125g (4oz) golden caster sugar
4 eggs
125g (4oz) plain flour
1 level tbsp instant espresso
 granules dissolved in
  2 tsp boiling water

FOR THE FROSTING
250g (8oz) mascarpone
125g (4oz) golden icing sugar, sifted
1 tbsp Marsala wine
cocoa powder, to decorate
icing sugar, to decorate

Preheat the oven to 200°C/fan 180°C/ gas mark 6, and line a cupcake tin with paper cases.

Put the butter in a heatproof bowl and melt in the microwave or in a heatproof bowl placed over a saucepan of barely simmering water, making sure the bowl does not touch the surface of the water.

Put the sugar and eggs in another bowl and, ideally using a free-standing mixer or an electric hand whisk, cream them together until light and frothy and doubled in volume – this will take several minutes.

Sift the flour and gently fold half of it into the mixture. Mix the coffee into the melted butter and pour half of this into the mixture. Add the remaining flour, followed by the rest of the coffee and butter mix. Gently fold these in.

Divide the mixture between the paper cases and bake for 25 minutes, or until a skewer inserted into the centre of a cupcake comes out clean. Leave to cool in the tin for 5 minutes and then turn the cupcakes out on a wire rack and allow to cool completely.

To make the frosting: whisk the mascarpone with the golden icing sugar, then add the Marsala and mix until combined. Spread this on top of each cupcake and finish with a generous dusting of cocoa powder and icing sugar on top.

Dark chocolate and coffee always make a good combination, so I've put these two fabulous flavours together to create the most delicious cupcakes.

MOCHA
CUPCAKES

MAKES 12 CUPCAKES

175g (6oz) unsalted butter, softened
175g (6oz) caster sugar
3 eggs
1 tbsp hot water mixed with 1 tsp
    instant coffee
150g (5oz) plain flour
25g (1oz) cocoa powder

FOR THE FROSTING
100g (3½oz) unsalted butter,
    softened
150g (5oz) icing sugar
2 tsp fresh coffee, ideally espresso,
    cooled
50g (2oz) melted dark chocolate
chocolate coffee beans, to decorate
edible gold paint, to decorate
    (optional, see page 159 for
    stockists)

Preheat the oven to 200°C/fan 180°C/ gas mark 6, and line a cupcake tin with paper cases.

Cream the butter and sugar together until light and fluffy, then add the eggs one at the time, beating well after each addition until combined and the mixture is smooth. Stir in the coffee mixture. Sift the flour and cocoa powder over the mixture and fold in.

Divide the mixture between the paper cases and bake for 20 minutes, or until a skewer inserted into the centre of a cupcake comes out clean. Leave to cool in the tin for 5 minutes and then turn the cupcakes out on a wire rack and allow to cool completely.

To make the frosting: beat the butter and icing sugar together until pale and fluffy. Add the coffee and melted chocolate, and beat until smooth. Pipe or spoon this on the top of each cupcake and finish by decorating with some chocolate coffee beans that have been lightly painted with edible gold paint.

This powerful recipe will give any afternoon tea or party a punchy start! The addition of the preserved stem ginger makes this little wonder very moist and moreish.

STEM GINGER CUPCAKES

MAKES 18 CUPCAKES

250g (8oz) unsalted butter
250g (8oz) dark brown soft sugar
250g (8oz) black treacle
300ml (½ pint) milk
3 eggs, lightly beaten
100g (3½oz) preserved stem
    ginger, drained and finely
    chopped, plus extra to
    decorate
400g (13oz) plain flour
2 tsp baking powder
1 tsp mixed spice
2 tsp ground ginger
1½ quantities Vanilla Buttercream
    Frosting (see page 88)

Preheat the oven to 200°C/fan 180°C/ gas mark 6, and line a 12-hole and a 6-hole cupcake tin with paper cases.

Put the butter, sugar and treacle in a saucepan and heat gently for about 5 minutes until the butter and sugar have melted. Stir in the milk and leave to cool before beating in the eggs.

Mix the chopped ginger and remaining ingredients together in a large bowl. Pour in the melted mixture and, using a wooden spoon, mix together to form a smooth thick batter.

Divide the mixture between the paper cases and bake for about 25 minutes, or until a skewer inserted into the centre of a cupcake comes out clean. Leave to cool in the tins for 5 minutes then transfer to a wire rack and allow to cool completely before frosting.

I like to finish mine with Vanilla Buttercream Frosting, and with some more finely chopped stem ginger sprinkled on the top.

This light and fruity cupcake has just the right balance of the tea flavour. The delicate Italian glacé fruits have been soaked in orange liqueur and look like jewels on top, adding a splash of glamour.

LADY GREY CUPCAKES

MAKES 12 CUPCAKES

150g (5oz) mixed glacé fruit, finely chopped, plus extra to decorate
2–3 tbsp orange liqueur
200ml (7fl oz) water
2 Lady Grey tea bags
2 eggs
200g (7oz) golden caster sugar
125ml (4fl oz) vegetable oil
1 tsp vanilla extract
250g (8oz) plain flour
½ tsp baking powder

FOR THE TOPPING
1 quantity Cream Cheese Frosting (see page 89)
edible gold leaf (see page 159 for stockists)

The day before you want to bake, in a small bowl, mix together the chopped glacé fruits and the orange liqueur, and leave to soak overnight.

Bring the water to the boil and pour it over the tea bags in a small bowl. Leave to infuse to create a strong tea. Allow to cool.

Preheat the oven to 200°C/fan 180°C/gas mark 6, and line a cupcake tin with paper cases.

In a large bowl, beat the eggs and gradually add the sugar while still beating. Continue beating while slowly pouring in the oil. Stir in the vanilla extract. Sift the flour and baking powder together. Fold these into the mixture a little at a time, alternating with additions of some of the strong tea, until the mixture is nice and smooth.

Drain the glacé fruits, reserving the orange liqueur. Fold the fruits into the cake mixture and divide the mixture between the paper cases. Bake for 20 minutes, or until a skewer inserted into a cupcake comes out clean. Once the cupcakes have cooked and whilst still warm, pierce their tops several times with a cocktail stick and spoon over the reserved orange liqueur. Leave to cool in the tin before decorating.

Pipe Cream Cheese Frosting on top of each cupcake and decorate with flecks of edible gold leaf to finish.

If you enjoy the rich flavour of liquorice, this recipe is for you. I like using these cupcakes as my base for Halloween cakes because of the natural dark colour of the sponge and icing.

LIQUORICE CUPCAKES

MAKES 16 CUPCAKES

100g (3½oz) pure liquorice sweets
185ml (6½fl oz) milk
250g (8oz) unsalted butter, softened
50g (2oz) dark muscovado sugar
4 eggs
185g (7½oz) self-raising flour
60g (2½oz) plain flour

FOR THE LIQUORICE FROSTING

100g (3½oz) pure liquorice
    sweets, plus some strands to
    decorate
50g (2oz) icing sugar
50g (2oz) unsalted butter, softened

Preheat the oven to 200°C/fan 180°C/ gas mark 6, and line a 12-hole and a 4-hole cupcake tin with paper cases.

Place the liquorice sweets and the milk in a saucepan and heat gently, stirring, until the sweets have dissolved. Leave to cool.

Place the butter and sugar in a bowl and cream together until pale and creamy. Add the eggs one at a time, beating well after each addition until well combined and the mixture is smooth. Sift the flours together and fold into the mixture together with the cool liquorice milk. Stir until smooth.

Divide the mixture between the paper cases to fill them three-quarters full and bake for 20 minutes, or until a skewer inserted into the centre of a cupcake comes out clean. Leave to cool in the tins for 5 minutes then transfer to a wire rack and allow to cool completely before frosting.

To make the Liquorice Frosting; place the liquorice sweets in a heatproof bowl and place over a saucepan of barely simmering water, making sure the bowl does not touch the surface of the water. Heat until completely dissolved, stirring occasionally. Remove from the heat and allow to cool.

Using a whisk, whip the icing sugar and butter together until pale and smooth. Still mixing, add in the dissolved liquorice and beat until smooth.

Pipe or spoon the frosting on top of the cooled cupcakes and decorate with strands of liquorice.

This is a classic cupcake that could be a safe base for any topping – and we all have a day when a good simple vanilla cupcake does the trick!

MADAGASCAN VANILLA CUPCAKES

MAKES 12 CUPCAKES

250g (8oz) unsalted butter, softened
250g (8oz) caster sugar
4 eggs
1 tsp vanilla extract, preferably
  Madagascan
185g (6½oz) self-raising flour
60g (2½oz) plain flour
185ml (6½fl oz) milk
1 quantity Vanilla Buttercream
  Frosting (see page 88) or Cream
  Cheese Frosting (see page 89)
sugar cake decorations, to decorate

Preheat the oven to 200°C/fan 180°C/gas mark 6, and line a cupcake tin with paper cases.

Place the butter and sugar in a bowl and cream together until pale and creamy. Add the eggs, one at a time, then add the vanilla extract and beat until well combined. Sift in the flours together and fold in, a little at a time, alternating with some of the milk. Stir until smooth.

Divide the mixture between the paper cases and bake for 20 minutes, or until a skewer inserted into the centre of a cupcake comes out clean. Leave to cool in the tin for 5 minutes, then transfer to a wire rack and allow to cool completely before frosting.

Pipe Vanilla Buttercream Frosting or Cream Cheese Frosting on top, and sprinkle over sugar decorations to finish.

One of the most popular flavours in Brittany, where I come from, is salted butter caramel. I grew up eating ice cream, sweets and spreads flavoured by this now very fashionable combination. These cupcakes are so decadent with a rich caramel sauce poured over the top.

SALTED BUTTER CARAMEL CUPCAKES

MAKES 12 CUPCAKES

175g (6oz) self-raising flour
1 tsp bicarbonate of soda
75g (3oz) unsalted butter, softened
100g (3½oz) muscovado sugar
2 eggs, lightly beaten
1 tsp vanilla extract
2 tbsp milk
50g (2oz) toffee or fudge pieces, chopped small

FOR THE CARAMEL SAUCE

125g (4oz) caster sugar
75g (3oz) salted butter
5 tbsp double cream
1 tsp vanilla extract

FOR THE BUTTERCREAM FROSTING

150g (5oz) unsalted butter, softened
150g (5oz) icing sugar
1 tsp vanilla extract
1 tsp caramel extract (optional)
few flakes of sea salt, to decorate

Preheat the oven to 200°C/fan 180°C/gas mark 6, and line a cupcake tin with paper cases.

Sift the flour and bicarbonate of soda together into a bowl and set aside. Using a free-standing mixer or an electric hand whisk, cream together the butter and sugar together for a good 5 minutes until very light and fluffy. Add the beaten eggs gradually, beating between each addition and adding 1 tablespoon of flour about halfway through to prevent curdling. Beat in the vanilla extract. Lastly fold in the remaining flour, the milk and the toffee/fudge pieces.

Divide the mixture between the paper cases and bake for 15–20 minutes, or until the tops spring back when pressed with a finger. Leave to cool in the tin for 5 minutes, then transfer to a wire rack and allow to cool completely.

To make the Caramel Sauce; dissolve the sugar in 4 tablespoons of water in a small heavy-based saucepan over a gentle heat. Increase the heat and simmer until you have a nice blonde caramel. Immediately remove from the heat. Add the butter, taking care as it may splutter. Keep stirring as you add the cream and vanilla extract, until smooth. Leave to cool.

To make the Buttercream Frosting; cream the butter and icing sugar together for at least 5 minutes and beat in the vanilla and caramel extracts.

Use a small palette knife to spread Buttercream Frosting on top of the cupcakes. Pour a little Caramel Sauce over the top, and sprinkle with a few sea salt flakes to finish.

Since travelling more often to the Far East, I have really begun to enjoy the taste of Asian food. The fusion of sweet and sour flavours works so well in traditional Asian cooking, and in these delicious cupcakes, too.

FUSION CUPCAKES

MAKES 12 CUPCAKES

5cm (2 inch) piece of fresh root ginger, peeled
2 lemon grass stalks, trimmed and roughly chopped
2 tsp vanilla extract
100g (3½oz) butter, softened
175g (6oz) golden caster sugar
2 eggs
200g (7oz) self-raising flour
125ml (4fl oz) milk

FOR THE FROSTING
100g (3½oz) butter, softened
350g (11½oz) icing sugar
3 tbsp milk
1 tsp vanilla extract
100g (3½oz) mixed exotic dried fruits (such as mango, coconut or pineapple), to decorate

Preheat the oven to 200°C/fan 180°C/gas mark 6, and line a cupcake tin with paper cases.

Place the ginger, lemon grass and vanilla extract in a food processor and process until you get a fine paste. Push through a sieve to extract the juice and discard the pulp.

Cream the butter and sugar together until light and fluffy. Add the reserved juice, then add the eggs one at a time, beating slowly until just combined. Add the flour and milk in alternate batches and stir with a wooden spoon until just combined.

Divide the mixture between the paper cases and bake for 15–20 minutes, or until a skewer inserted into the centre of a cupcake comes out clean. Leave to cool in the tin for 5 minutes, then transfer to a wire rack and allow to cool completely before frosting.

To make the frosting; beat the butter until very pale, then gradually beat in the icing sugar. Add the milk and vanilla extract and beat until well combined.

Use a small palette knife or piping bag to decorate the cakes with the frosting. Roughly chop the dried fruit and arrange on top.

One of my favourite things about the arrival of gastropubs is the rebirth of proper English 'puds'. When properly made, they are rich, filling and so indulgent. This one is my winter perfection and, because the cakes are cute and tiny, you won't feel guilty about eating them. These actually need to be made in smaller standard cupcake cases and not the larger 'muffin' type.

STICKY TOFFEE CUPCAKES

MAKES 12 STANDARD CUPCAKES

150ml (¼ pint) hot water
1 tea bag
50g (2oz) dried apricots, roughly chopped
50g (2oz) dates, stoned and roughly chopped
150g (5oz) self-raising flour
1 tsp baking powder
50g (2oz) muscovado sugar
1 tbsp golden syrup
2 large eggs, lightly beaten
50g (2oz) butter, melted

FOR THE TOFFEE SAUCE
50g (2oz) caster sugar
50g (2oz) butter
100ml (3½fl oz) double cream
pouring cream, to serve

Preheat the oven to 200°C/fan 180°C/gas mark 6, and line a standard bun tin with paper cases.

Put the hot water, tea bag, apricots and dates in a saucepan, bring to the boil, then remove from the heat and leave to soak and cool.

Sift the flour and baking powder together into a large mixing bowl. Drain the fruits, then add them to the flour with the muscovado sugar, golden syrup, eggs and butter, then mix together until blended.

Divide the mixture between the paper cases and bake for 25–30 minutes, or until a skewer inserted into the centre of a cupcake comes out clean.

Towards the end of the cupcake cooking time, make the toffee sauce: heat the caster sugar in a heavy-based saucepan until you get a dark caramel. Add the butter, stirring well with a wooden spoon. Deglaze the pan by stirring in the double cream. When all the caramel has dissolved, pass the sauce through a sieve into a warm serving jug.

When the cupcakes are cooked, carefully remove the paper cases and serve immediately, piping hot, with the toffee sauce and lots of pouring cream.

NUTTY & CHOCOLATEY CUPCAKES

FRUITY CUPCAKES

RICH & SPICY CUPCAKES

GUILT-FREE CUPCAKES

STYLING CUPCAKES

COOKIES

BARS & BISCUITS

4

This fat-free sponge recipe is very light and delicate… like an angel! The raspberry frosting adds a great fruity touch to these cupcakes, making them perfect for summer.

ANGEL FOOD CUPCAKES WITH RASPBERRY FROSTING

MAKES 12 CUPCAKES

115g (3½oz) plain flour
85g (3¼oz) icing sugar
1 tsp cream of tartar
8 egg whites
pinch of salt
150g (5oz) caster sugar
½ tsp vanilla extract
½ tsp almond extract

FOR THE RASPBERRY FROSTING

100g (3½oz) fresh raspberries,
    plus extra to decorate
125g (4oz) unsalted butter, softened
    and diced
225g (7½oz) icing sugar, sifted,
    plus more to decorate

Preheat the oven to 200°C/fan 180°C/gas mark 6, and line a cupcake tin with paper cases.

Sift the flour, icing sugar and cream of tartar into a bowl and set aside. In a large bowl whisk the egg whites until frothy, ideally using a free-standing mixer or an electric hand whisk. Then add the salt and gradually begin to add the caster sugar a tablespoonful at a time. Continue whisking until stiff peaks form – this will take several minutes.

Stir in the vanilla and almond extracts, then add the flour and icing sugar mixture. Fold the mixture gently with a large metal spoon until combined. It's important to do this quickly – if the mixture is left to stand, it will collapse and spoil the light consistency of the cakes.

Divide the mixture between the paper cases and bake for 15–20 minutes, or until a skewer inserted into the centre of a cupcake comes out clean. Leave to cool in the tin for 5 minutes, then transfer to a wire rack and allow to cool completely. These cakes will sink a little as they cool.

To make the Raspberry Frosting; rub the raspberries through a fine-meshed sieve to yield about 2 tablespoons of raspberry purée. Add the butter to a clean bowl and cream until soft. Sift some of the icing sugar over the top, then beat in to combine. Repeat this process until all the sugar has been incorporated into the butter. Then beat in the raspberry purée to give a spreading consistency.

Using a piping bag with a plain nozzle, pipe the frosting (see page 98 for piping tips), and decorate with fresh raspberries and a dusting of icing sugar.

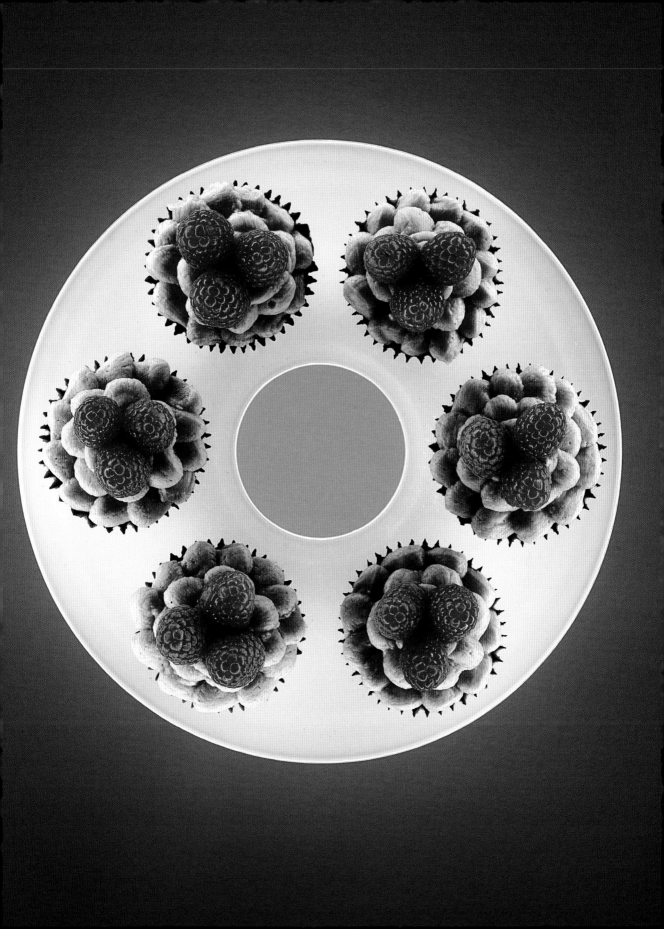

I think that if I was on a diet, I would miss chocolate the most. But don't worry, you can spoil yourself with this recipe… but not too often!

LOW-FAT CHOCOLATE CUPCAKES

MAKES 12 CUPCAKES

100g (3½oz) plain flour
25g (1oz) cocoa powder
4 large eggs
125g (4oz) caster sugar
25g (1oz) chocolate chips

FOR THE TOPPING

75g (3oz) low-fat spread
150g (5oz) low-fat cream cheese
100g (3½oz) dark chocolate (70% cocoa solids), melted and cooled
artificial sweetener, to taste

Preheat the oven to 200°C/fan 180°C/ gas mark 6, and line a cupcake tin with paper cases.

Sift together the flour and cocoa powder. In a large bowl, whisk together the eggs and sugar using an electric hand whisk until the mixture becomes thick, foamy and has doubled in size. This may take up to 10 minutes, but it is worth it, as the more air that gets in the lighter the sponge will be. Gently fold in the flour and cocoa powder followed by the chocolate chips, taking care to knock out as little air as possible.

Divide the mixture between the paper cases and bake for 20 minutes, or until a skewer inserted into the centre of a cupcake comes out clean. Leave to cool in the tin for 5 minutes, then transfer to a wire rack and allow to cool completely.

To make the topping: mix the low-fat spread with the cream cheese, then stir in the cooled melted chocolate. Sweeten to taste with the artificial sweetener, then spread over the top of the cupcakes.

As much as I always try not to compromise on ingredients, it is possible to still indulge yourself even if you are following a low-fat diet. Despite being low in fat, these cupcakes are delicious, light and tasty. They won't make you feel guilty and one is much more enjoyable than an apple!

LOW-FAT WHITE CHOCOLATE & BERRY CUPCAKES

MAKES 12 CUPCAKES

100g (3½oz) low-fat spread
100g (3½oz) golden caster sugar
175g (6oz) self-raising flour, sifted
2 eggs
½ tsp vanilla extract
4 tbsp skimmed milk

FOR THE WHITE CHOCOLATE TOPPING

50g (2oz) white chocolate, broken into pieces
150g (5oz) low-fat cream cheese
2 tbsp icing sugar, plus more to decorate
200g (7oz) mixed raspberries, blueberries and redcurrants, for decorating
white chocolate curls, to decorate

Preheat the oven to 200°C/fan 180°C/gas mark 6, and line a cupcake tin with paper cases.

Put all the cake ingredients in a large mixing bowl and beat for 2–3 minutes, ideally using an electric hand whisk, until pale and fluffy.

Divide the mixture between the paper cases and bake for 18–20 minutes, or until a skewer inserted into the centre of a cupcake comes out clean. Leave to cool in the tin for 5 minutes and then turn the cupcakes out on a wire rack and allow to cool completely.

To make the White Chocolate Topping: put the white chocolate in a large heatproof bowl and place over a saucepan of barely simmering water, making sure the bowl does not touch the surface of the water. Heat until completely melted. Allow to cool slightly, then beat in the cream cheese and icing sugar until smooth. Chill in the refrigerator until it firms up a little.

Using a small palette knife or piping bag, cover the cupcakes with the topping. Decorate with the berries, dust with icing sugar and top with white chocolate curls.

Yes, it is possible – these dainty cupcakes are fat-free and delicious, too. The crystallized flowers give them a perfect look for a chic afternoon treat.

FAT-FREE JASMINE & VIOLET CUPCAKES

MAKES 12 CUPCAKES

FOR THE CRYSTALLIZED FLOWERS
a few violet and jasmine flowers
1 egg white, lightly beaten
2 tbsp granulated sugar

3 eggs
75g (3oz) golden caster sugar
75g (3oz) self-raising flour
1 tsp vanilla extract
2 drops of vanilla essence

FOR THE JASMINE DRIZZLE
1 jasmine tea bag
3 tbsp boiling water
250g (8oz) icing sugar

First make the crystallized edible flowers; dip the violet and jasmine flowers in the beaten egg white, then sprinkle them all over with granulated sugar. Leave them to dry on greaseproof paper overnight.

Preheat the oven to 200°C/fan 180°C/gas mark 6, and line a cupcake tin with paper cases.

In a large bowl whisk the eggs and sugar together until light, fluffy and doubled in volume, using an electric hand whisk. Sift the flour and gently fold it into the mixture, followed by the vanilla extract and essence.

Divide the mixture between the paper cases and bake for 20 minutes, or until a skewer inserted into a cupcake comes out clean. Leave to cool in the tin for 5 minutes, then transfer to a wire rack and allow to cool completely.

To make the Jasmine Drizzle; put the tea bag in a small heatproof bowl and pour the boiling water over it. Leave to infuse until the tea is nice and strong, then remove the tea bag. Mix the icing sugar into the tea until you get a nice thick drizzling consistency. Drizzle over the cooled cupcakes and, before it sets, decorate with the crystallized violets and jasmine flowers.

These cupcakes are based on my favourite French pear dessert, Tarte Bordaloue. There is, of course, no pastry in this version and, being gluten-free, it is perfect for anyone with a gluten allergy.

GLUTEN-FREE PEAR & ALMOND CUPCAKES

MAKES 12 CUPCAKES

300g (10oz) ground almonds
1 tbsp gluten-free baking powder
100g (3½oz) caster sugar
100g (3½oz) butter, melted
2 eggs, beaten
250ml (8fl oz) milk
3 canned baby pears, drained
25g (1oz) flaked almonds
icing sugar, to decorate

FOR THE POACHED PEARS

2 large ripe pears, peeled, cored
   and quartered
100g (3½oz) caster sugar
200ml (7fl oz) water
1 vanilla pod, split lengthways

If time allows poach the pears the day before. Put the sugar, water and vanilla pod in a saucepan. Slowly bring to the boil, stirring, until the sugar has dissolved. Add the pear quarters, cover and simmer over a low heat for 15 minutes. Leave to cool.

When you are ready to cook the cupcakes, preheat the oven to 200°C/fan 180°C/gas mark 6, and line a cupcake tin with paper cases.

In a large bowl, mix together the ground almonds, baking powder and sugar. Add the melted butter, eggs and milk, and mix until creamy. Drain the poached pears and cut them into small cubes, then fold these into the mixture.

Divide the mixture between the paper cases. Chop each of the canned baby pears into quarters (you should have 12 pieces) and place one quarter upright standing proud on top of each cake. Sprinkle over the flaked almonds and bake for 25–30 minutes, or until a skewer inserted into the centre of a cupcake comes out clean. Leave to cool in the tin for 5 minutes, then transfer to a wire rack and allow to cool completely. Dust with icing sugar before serving.

These energy-packed cupcakes are perfect for kids' lunch boxes or for a healthy treat or snack to help keep you going through the day.

GRANOLA & MIXED SPICE CUPCAKES

MAKES 12 CUPCAKES

225g (7½oz) wholemeal flour
100g (3½oz) granola, plus an
    extra 75g (3oz) for the topping
2 tsp baking powder
1 tsp mixed spice
1 tbsp poppy seeds
150g (5oz) dried apricots, chopped
50g (2oz) golden sultanas
3 tbsp sunflower oil
2 eggs
175ml (6fl oz) milk
100ml (3½oz) clear honey

Preheat the oven to 200°C/fan 180°C/ gas mark 6, and line a cupcake tin with paper cases.

In a large mixing bowl, mix together the flour, 100g (3½oz) of granola, the baking powder, mixed spice, poppy seeds and dried fruit.

In another bowl, whisk together the oil, eggs, milk and honey until well blended. Pour into the dry ingredients and quickly stir.

Divide between the paper cases and sprinkle over the remaining granola. Bake for 25 minutes, or until a skewer inserted into a cupcake comes out clean. Leave to cool in the tin for 5 minutes, then transfer to a wire rack and allow to cool completely.

They will keep in the fridge for 2–3 days, or can be frozen.

These flour-free cupcakes are perfect for people who have a gluten allergy. The decadent addition of ground almonds make these little cakes very moist, and the final drizzle of spicy syrup gives them a great tasty touch.

GLUTEN-FREE PROVENÇAL ORANGE CUPCAKES

MAKES 12 CUPCAKES

175g (6oz) ground almonds
150g (5oz) caster sugar
2 tsp gluten-free baking powder
4 eggs, beaten
200ml (7fl oz) sunflower oil
finely grated zest of 1 lemon
finely grated zest of 2 oranges,
   ideally Seville, plus a few extra
   strands to decorate

FOR THE SYRUP
juice of 1 lemon
juice of 2 oranges, ideally Seville
100g (3½oz) caster sugar
pinch of ground cloves
2 tsp ground cinnamon

Preheat the oven to 200°C/fan 180°C/ gas mark 6, and line a cupcake tin with paper cases.

In a mixing bowl, combine the ground almonds, caster sugar and baking powder. Add the eggs and oil, and mix gently together. Stir the lemon and orange zest into the mixture.

Divide the mixture between the paper cases and bake for 30 minutes, or until a skewer inserted into the centre of a cupcake comes out clean. Leave to cool in the tin for 5 minutes, then transfer to a wire rack and allow to cool slightly.

To make the syrup: pour the lemon and orange juices into a small saucepan. Add the sugar, cloves and cinnamon. Bring to the boil, then reduce the heat and simmer for 3 minutes.

Once the cupcakes have cooked but whilst still warm, pierce their tops several times with a cocktail stick. Spoon the syrup over the cakes and allow it to soak in whilst they cool. Decorate with strands of orange zest to finish.

These breakfast cupcakes make a tasty and nourishing kick-start to any day. I like to eat mine straight from the oven with honey, as you then get all the hearty flavour.

COURGETTE CUPCAKES

MAKES 12 CUPCAKES

250g (8oz) wholemeal flour
2 tsp baking powder
1 tsp mixed spices
100g (3½oz) mixed seeds (such as
    pumpkin, sesame, sunflower)
2 eggs
200ml (7fl oz) milk
4 tsp vegetable oil
4 tsp clear honey
150g (5oz) courgettes, grated
clear honey and Greek-style
    yoghurt, to serve (optional)

Preheat the oven to 200°C/fan 180°C/ gas mark 6, and line a cupcake tin with paper cases.

In a large mixing bowl, thoroughly mix together all the dry ingredients (but do not sift the flour, as we want to keep all the goodness from the wholemeal.) Add all the liquid ingredients and mix until nice and smooth. Fold in the courgette, taking care not to break it up.

Divide the mixture between the paper cases and bake for 25 minutes or until a skewer inserted into a cupcake comes out clean. Leave to cool in the tin for 5 minutes, then transfer to a wire rack and allow to cool completely.

To serve, drizzle with clear honey and some yoghurt if liked.

5

This frosting can be tinted by using natural food colouring. I prefer to use an edible paste colouring rather than a liquid, as it doesn't affect the consistency of the frosting.

VANILLA BUTTERCREAM FROSTING

FOR 12 CUPCAKES

250g (8oz) unsalted butter, softened
500g (1lb) icing sugar
2 tbsp milk
1 tsp vanilla extract

In a large bowl, cream the butter, ideally using an electric hand whisk on medium speed. Blend in the sugar, a quarter of it at a time, beating well after each addition. Beat in the milk and vanilla extract, and continue mixing until light and fluffy.

Keep the frosting covered until you are ready to use it.

Using a small palette knife, smooth the frosting over the cupcakes. You can also create small spikes by quickly touching the frosting with the flat blade of the palette knife.

Be careful when melting white chocolate, as it is much more temperamental than dark.

CREAM CHEESE FROSTING

FOR 12 CUPCAKES

50g (2oz) white chocolate, broken into pieces
200g (7oz) cream cheese, softened
100g (3½oz) unsalted butter, softened
1 tsp vanilla extract
500g (1lb) icing sugar

Put the chocolate pieces in a heatproof bowl and place over a saucepan of barely simmering water making sure the bowl does not touch the surface of the water. Stir until the chocolate melts and is smooth. Allow to cool to room temperature.

In a bowl, using a wooden spoon or electric hand whisk, beat together the cream cheese and butter until smooth. Mix in the melted white chocolate and the vanilla extract. Gradually beat in the icing sugar until the mixture is fluffy.

Using a small palette knife, smooth the frosting over the cupcakes. You can also create small spikes by quickly touching the frosting with the flat blade of the palette knife.

Use Britsh Lion Standard egg whites. If you are worried about using raw eggs, you can buy reconstituted albumen powder instead.

ROYAL ICING

MAKES 500G (1LB 2OZ)

2 egg whites
1 tsp lemon juice
about 500g (1lb 2oz) icing sugar,
  sifted
edible food colouring paste (see
  page 159 for stockists)

Tip the egg whites into a bowl and stir in the lemon juice. Gradually add the sieved icing sugar, mixing well after each addition.

Continue adding small amounts of icing sugar until you achieve the desired consistency. For piping, the icing should be fairly stiff.

Edible food colouring paste is highly concentrated so only use a tiny amount. Dip a cocktail stick into the colouring paste. Mix well before adding more colouring paste to avoid streaks.

Use good-quality dark chocolate to make this rich chocolate buttercream frosting. A great topping for any chocolate cupcakes or cakes.

CHOCOLATE FROSTING

FOR 12 CUPCAKES

200ml (7fl oz) single cream
250g (8oz) dark chocolate, finely
    chopped
50g (2oz) unsalted butter, softened

Heat the cream in a small saucepan, but do not allow it to boil.

Put the chocolate in a heatproof bowl and pour the hot cream over it through a fine sieve. Gently stir the cream into the chocolate until the mixture is nice and glossy. Gently mix in the soft butter. Leave to cool completely.

Once it is cool, ideally using an electric hand whisk, beat until nice and fluffy.

Use to fill or top cupcakes or cakes. You can use this without the final whipping to give a dark glossy chocolate coating.

**FOR 12 MINI CUPCAKES
YOU WILL NEED:**

rose mould, approximately
   the same diameter as your
   cupcakes (see page 159 for
   stockists)
cornflour, for dusting
chocolate paste or 'plastic',
   coloured with red and pink
   edible food colouring paste
   (see page 159 for stockists)
small paintbrush
boiled water, cooled
edible glitter in 'disco red' and
   'plum perfection' (see page
   159 for stockists)
piping bag with small star-
   tipped nozzle
½ quantity Vanilla Buttercream
   or Cream Cheese Frosting
   (see pages 88–9), coloured
   with red or pink edible food
   colouring pastes
12 mini cupcakes

Dust the inside of the mould with a little cornflour to stop the chocolate 'plastic' from sticking.

Dab your fingertips into the cornflour, take a small ball of chocolate 'plastic' and press tightly into the mould.

Pop out the rose shape – it will not set hard so there is no need to leave it to dry.

Using a small dry paintbrush, brush off the excess cornflour from the rose shapes, then lightly brush the surface with the cooled boiled water.

Sprinkle red or pink glitter over, shake off the excess, and leave to dry. Using a piping bag with a star-tipped nozzle, pipe spirals of frosting on to each cupcake and top with a rose. Repeat for the remaining cupcakes

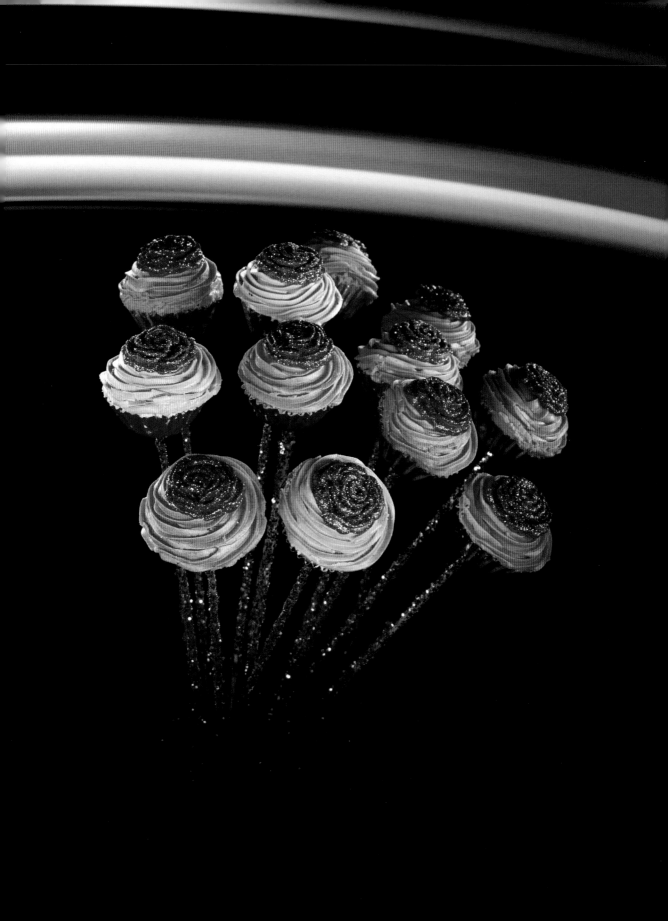

FOR 12 CUPCAKES
YOU WILL NEED:

cornflour, for dusting

small rolling pin

50g (2oz) white ready-made
     sugar flower paste icing (see
     page 159 for stockists)

small dry paintbrush

edible rainbow dust in
     'Christmas red' (see page
     159 for stockists)

boiled water, cooled

100g (3½oz) desiccated coconut

small palette knife

1 quantity Vanilla Buttercream
     or Cream Cheese Frosting
     (see pages 88–9), coloured
     with green edible food
     colouring paste

12 chocolate or vanilla cupcake
     bases (see pages 16 and 66)

BUNNY CUPCAKES

Dust a little cornflour over your work surface and roll out the petal paste icing very thinly, about 2mm (⅛ inch) thick. Cut out 24 petal shapes for ears, each 8cm (3½ inches) long and 2cm (¾ inch) at the widest part (you may want to make a paper template to cut around). Leave to dry in the refrigerator for several hours or overnight, until hard.

Using a small dry paintbrush, stain one side of each ear with red edible rainbow dust, leaving a white border.

Lightly paint the white areas only of each ear on both sides with cooled boiled water and immediately dip into the desiccated coconut to coat. Leave to dry for a few minutes.

Using a small palette knife, spread the frosting over each cake. Create a spiky grass effect by tapping the flat blade of the palette knife on to the frosting. Poke 2 ears into each cake to finish.

FOR 12 CUPCAKES
YOU WILL NEED:

cornflour, for dusting

small rolling pin

40g (1½oz) white ready-made
    sugar flower paste icing (see
    page 159 for stockists)

15cm (6-inch) square of
    greaseproof paper

50g (2oz) Royal Icing (see
    page 90)

small paintbrush

boiled water, cooled

edible glitter in gold, blue and
    red (see page 159 for
    stockists)

small palette knife

1 quantity Vanilla Buttercream
    or Cream Cheese Frosting
    (see pages 88–9), coloured
    with violet edible food
    colouring paste (see page
    159 for stockists)

12 chocolate or vanilla cupcake
    bases (see pages 16 and 66)

CROWN
CUPCAKES

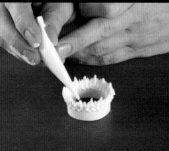

Dust a little cornflour over your work surface to stop the icing from sticking, and roll out the sugar flower paste 5mm (¼inch) thick. Cut 12 strips, each 15cm (6 inches) long and 1cm (½inch) wide. Press the two ends together to make a circle, and leave to dry in the refrigerator for several hours or ideally overnight until hard.

Make a mini piping bag with the greaseproof paper by rolling it into a cone and folding the edges over. Fill with royal icing and snip off the tip so the icing flows. Pipe a row of small dots on top of the rim of the crown, holding the bag vertically with the tip close to the surface, squeeze a little icing out then pushing down and up sharply to finish. Pipe a second row of dots on top of the first row in between the gaps, then more dots to build up the tips of the crown. Leave to dry for a few minutes.

Lightly brush all over with the cooled boiled water and sprinkle with gold edible glitter. Use a small paintbrush to paint on additional colours as desired.

Using a small palette knife, spread the frosting on top of each cake. (If your frosting seems a little too thick, dip your palette knife in hot water and this will make spreading easier.) Top with a glittering crown.

FOR 12 CUPCAKES

YOU WILL NEED:

1 quantity Vanilla Buttercream
or Cream Cheese Frosting
(see pages 88–9), coloured
with peach edible food
colouring paste

piping bag with a plain round
nozzle

12 chocolate or vanilla cupcake
bases (see pages 16 and 66)

edible diamonds, edible gold
balls, sugar flowers, to
decorate

tweezers

Your frosting needs to be free-flowing
and not too stiff for this decoration. Fill
the piping bag with frosting, twist the
end tightly and squeeze gently until the
frosting starts to come through. Starting
at the rim furthest away from you, hold
the piping bag at a 45° angle, pipe a
dot and stop squeezing, tipping the bag
vertically towards the centre of the cake.
Repeat around three-quarters of
the rim, then create a second row in
between the gaps, and keep repeating
until you reach the middle.

Continue piping dots down the back of
the cupcake to the rim. Repeat for the
remaining cupcakes.

Use tweezers to arrange your chosen
bling decorations carefully on top.

BLING
CUPCAKES

FOR 12 CUPCAKES
YOU WILL NEED:

100g (3½oz) white chocolate, melted, coloured with skin-coloured edible pastes

squeezy bottle

beach bum mould (see page 159 for stockists)

piping bag with a plain nozzle

1 quantity Vanilla Buttercream or Cream Cheese Frosting (see pages 88–9), coloured with yellow, violet or orange edible food colouring pastes

12 chocolate or vanilla cupcake bases (see pages 16 and 66)

small paintbrush

edible black food paint, or any colour of your choice (see page 159 for stockists)

CHEEKY CUPCAKES

Transfer the coloured white chocolate to a squeezy bottle for easy use or simply spoon the melted chocolate into the beach bum moulds, making sure they are full to the top. Tap the moulds on to the work surface to get rid of any air bubbles before leaving to set in the refrigerator for 1 hour.

Fill the piping bag with frosting, twist the end tightly and squeeze gently until the frosting starts to come through. Hold the bag vertically and slowly pipe a ring of icing around the rim of a cupcake, then continue in a spiral until you reach the centre. Stop squeezing, then push the bag down and up sharply to finish.

Pop the chocolate beach bums out of the moulds.

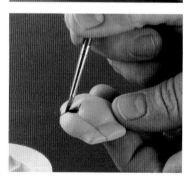

Using a small paintbrush, carefully paint on the bikini decoration using black edible paint (or the colouring of your choice). Leave to dry for a few minutes.

Place on top of the cupcakes to finish. Repeat with the remaining cupcakes.

FOR 12 CUPCAKES
YOU WILL NEED:

15cm (6 inch) square of
 greaseproof paper
½ quantity Vanilla Buttercream
 or Cream Cheese Frosting,
 (see pages 88–9), 25g (1oz)
 left white (for the nose), half
 the remainder coloured with
 beige edible food paste and
 the rest coloured brown
12 chocolate or vanilla cupcake
 bases (see pages 16 and 66)
2 piping bags with plain round
 nozzles
24 chocolate 'eyes' (see page
 159 for stockists)
6 mini marshmallows

HEDGEHOG CUPCAKES

Make a mini piping bag with the greaseproof paper by rolling it into a cone shape and folding the edges over. Fill with the white frosting and snip off the tip of the bag so the icing flows out. First, make the base of the nose by piping a 2cm (¾-inch) spiral of white frosting above the rim on each cupcake.

Fill one of the nozzled piping bags with beige-coloured frosting and the other with brown-coloured frosting, twist the ends tightly and squeeze gently until the frosting starts to come through. Take the beige piping bag, hold at a 45° angle and pipe outwards around half the rim of a cupcake, squeezing a little and tilting the bag upright to form the spikes.

Now take the brown frosting and pipe more spikes overlapping the beige spikes to form a second row. Repeat, alternating the colours to cover the cake until you reach the nose.

Position the chocolate 'eyes' into position above the nose.

Cut the corner off a mini marshmallow and place on top of the white frosting to form the tip of the nose. Repeat with the remaining cupcakes.

**FOR 12 CUPCAKES
YOU WILL NEED:**

small palette knife

1 quantity Vanilla Buttercream
   or Cream Cheese frosting
   (see pages 88–9), coloured
   with violet edible food
   colouring paste

12 chocolate or vanilla cupcake
   bases (see pages 16 and 66)

piping bag with a plain nozzle
   (about 5mm/¼ inch)

½ quantity Vanilla Buttercream
   or Cream CheeseFrosting,
   25g (1oz) coloured with
   black edible food colouring
   paste (for the stigma), the
   remainder coloured with
   orange edible food colouring
   paste

15cm (6-inch) square of
   greaseproof paper

Using a small palette knife, spread
the violet-coloured frosting over each
cupcake to cover.

Fill the nozzled piping bag with orange
frosting. Twist the end tightly and
squeeze gently until the frosting starts to
come through. Holding the bag at a 45°
angle, start at the rim and pipe a petal
shape by squeezing the bag across
the cake towards the centre and twist
upwards to finish. Repeat around the
cake to cover.

Repeat a second layer over the top of
first layer.

Make a mini piping bag with the
greaseproof paper by rolling it into a
cone shape and folding the edges
over. Fill with black frosting and snip
off the tip of the bag so the icing flows
out. Pipe small dots in the centre of the
cupcake to form the stigma, piling them
to build up some height. Repeat with the
remaining cupcakes.

SUMMER
FLOWER
CUPCAKES

**FOR 12 CUPCAKES
YOU WILL NEED:**

100g (3½oz) dark chocolate, melted

skull mould (see page 159 for stockists)

small paintbrush

edible glitter in silver and red (see page 159 for stockists)

piping bag with a plain nozzle

1 quantity Vanilla Buttercream or Cream Cheese Frosting (see pages 88–9), coloured with black edible food colouring paste

12 chocolate cupcake bases (see page 16)

Spoon the melted chocolate into the moulds, making sure they are full to the top. Tap the moulds on the work surface to get rid of any air bubbles before leaving to set in the refrigerator for 1 hour.

Pop the chocolate skulls out of the moulds. Using a small paintbrush, decorate with edible glitter.

Fill the piping bag with frosting, twist the end tightly and squeeze gently until the frosting starts to come through. Hold the bag vertically and slowly pipe a ring of icing around the edge of a cupcake, then continue in a spiral until you reach the centre and the cupcake is covered. Stop the pressure, then push the bag down and up sharply to finish.

Position a skull on top of each cupcake to finish. Repeat with the remaining cupcakes.

BLACK SKULL CAKES

FOR 12 CUPCAKES
YOU WILL NEED:

100g (3½oz) white chocolate, melted and coloured with skin-coloured edible food pastes

squeezy bottle

torso mould (see page 159 for stockists)

piping bag with a plain nozzle

1 quantity Vanilla Buttercream or Cream Cheese Frosting (see pages 88–9), coloured with caramel edible food colouring paste

125g (4oz) toffee chips

12 chocolate or vanilla cupcake bases (see pages 16 and 66)

spray edible confectioners' glaze (see page 159 for stockists)

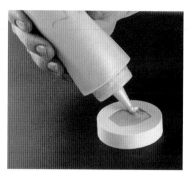

Transfer the melted chocolate to a squeezy bottle for easy use or spoon into the moulds, making sure they are full to the top. Tap the moulds on the work surface to get rid of any air bubbles before leaving to set in the refrigerator for 1 hour.

Fill the piping bag with frosting, twist the end tightly and squeeze gently until the frosting starts to come through. Hold the bag vertically and slowly pipe a ring of icing around the edge of a cupcake, then continue in a spiral until you reach the centre. Stop the pressure, then push the bag down and up sharply to finish. Sprinkle toffee chips around the rim. Pop the chocolate torsos out of the moulds.

Spray or paint on edible confectioners' glaze to give a shiny finish and place one on each cupcake to finish. Repeat with the remaining cupcakes.

MAN CAKES

FOR 12 CUPCAKES
YOU WILL NEED:

25g/¾oz Royal Icing (see
    page 90), coloured with
    skin-coloured edible food
    colouring paste
dome-shaped silicone cupcake
    mould
1½ quantities Vanilla
    Buttercream or Cream
    Cheese Frosting (see
    pages 88–9), coloured with
    skin-coloured edible food
    colouring paste
small palette knife

Make the nipples from 2 small circles
of royal icing and leave to set. Bake
vanilla or chocolate cupcake bases (as
on page 66 or 16) in the dome-shaped
silicone moulds without using cupcake
papers. Cut each cake in half vertically.

Spread a thin layer of frosting inside
one of the cut halves and sandwich
the other half together. Using a small
palette knife, spread frosting all over the
top of the cupcakes and smooth over.

Place a nipple on top of each cake
and serve on a tartlet tin or plate.

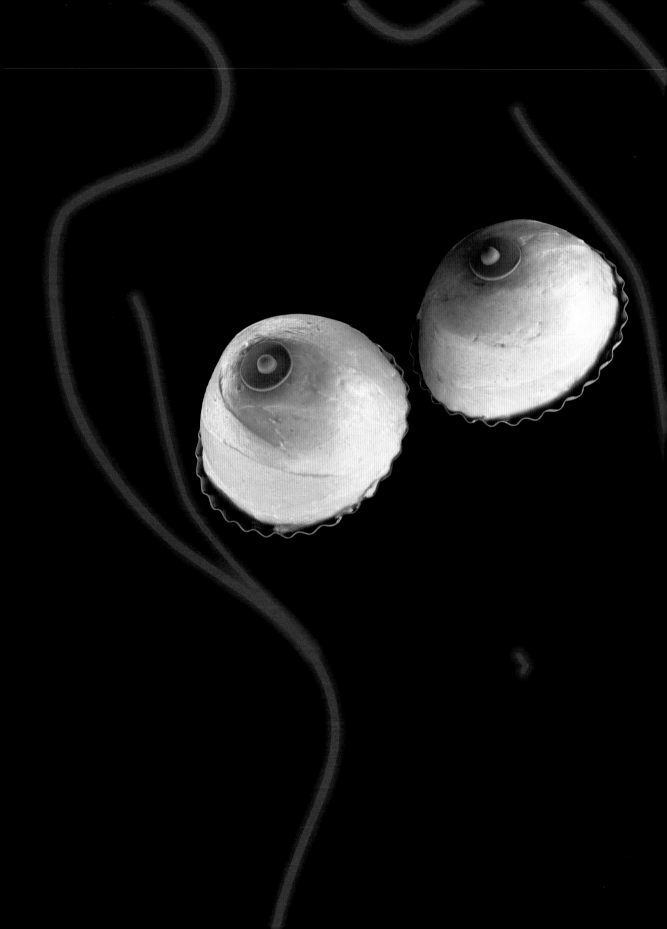

**FOR 12 CUPCAKES
YOU WILL NEED:**

100g (3½oz) white chocolate

12 dome-shaped chocolates
(such as Lindor)

small paintbrush

edible rainbow dust in red (see
page 159 for stockists)

boiled water, cooled

edible glitter in blue, green and
black (see page 159 for
stockists)

1 quantity Vanilla Buttercream
or Cream Cheese Frosting
(see pages 88–9), coloured
with edible colouring pastes

12 chocolate or vanilla cupcake
bases (see pages 16 and 66)

15cm (6-inch) square of
greaseproof paper

piping gel, coloured with red
edible colouring paste

POKE-IN-THE-EYE
CUPCAKES

Melt the white chocolate in a heatproof
bowl placed over a saucepan of barely
simmering water, making sure the
bowl does not touch the surface of the
water. Dip the chocolates in the white
chocolate until completely covered
and leave to set on a plate in the
refrigerator for 2 hours.

Using a small dry paintbrush, dust red
edible rainbow dust over the white
chocolate eyeballs.

Lightly brush a circle of water on one
side, then paint a ring using edible blue
and green glitter. Paint the centre with
black edible glitter.

Using the tip of a small sharp knife,
score from the centre of the eyeball
outwards several times to create a
veined effect. Spread frosting over the
cupcakes and place an eyeball on top.

Make a mini piping bag with the
greaseproof paper by rolling into a cone
shape and folding the edges over. Fill
with red piping gel and snip off the tip of
the bag so the icing flows out. Pipe the
gel into the centre of the eyeball and let
it drizzle down over the frosting. Repeat
with the remainng cupcakes.

FOR 12 CUPCAKES
YOU WILL NEED:

6 pieces of bubble wrap, each
10 x 20cm (4 x 8 inches)

200g (7oz) dark, milk or white
chocolate, melted

1 quantity Vanilla Buttercream
or Cream Cheese Frosting
(see pages 88–9)

12 chocolate cupcake bases
(see page 16)

small paintbrush with soft
bristles

edible rainbow dust in gold (see
page 159 for stockists)

edible glitter in gold (optional)

CHOCOLATE HONEYCOMB CUPCAKES

Wash and dry the bubble wrap and place on plates (or any flat surface that will fit in your refrigerator) with the bubbles face up. Pour the melted chocolate over the bubble wrap, dividing the chocolate equally between each piece.

Use a knife to spread the chocolate out, then leave to set in the refrigerator for 1 hour. Meanwhile, spread frosting on top of each cupcake.

Once the chocolate has set, carefully peel off and discard the bubble wrap.

Use a small dry paintbrush to highlight areas of the chocolate honeycomb with gold edible rainbow dust.

Then snap each chocolate piece into 4 so you have 24 pieces. Push 2 pieces into each cupcake and sprinkle a pinch of edible glitter down the sides of the frosting to finish.

FOR 12 CUPCAKES
YOU WILL NEED:

cornflour, for dusting

small rolling pin

40g (1½oz) white ready-made
    sugar flower paste icing

snowflake cutter (see page 159
    for stockists)

small paintbrush with soft
    bristles

boiled water, cooled

edible glitter in silver (see
    page 159 for stockists)

piping bag with a plain nozzle

1 quantity Vanilla Buttercream
    or Cream Cheese Frosting
    (see pages 88–9), coloured
    with red edible food
    colouring paste

12 chocolate or vanilla cupcake
    bases (see pages 16 and 66)

SNOWFLAKE CUPCAKES

Dust a little cornflour over your work surface to stop the icing from sticking, and roll out the sugar flower paste icing very thinly, about 2mm (¾ inch) thick.

Using a snowflake cutter, cut out 12 shapes and leave to dry in the refrigerator for several hours or ideally overnight, until hard.

Using a small paintbrush, lightly brush cooled boiled water over the surface of the snowflake. Cover with edible glitter and shake off the excess, then leave to dry for a few minutes.

Fill the piping bag with frosting, twist the end tightly and squeeze gently until the frosting starts to come through. Hold the bag vertically and slowly pipe a ring of icing around the edge of a cupcake, then continue in a spiral until you reach the centre and the cupcake is covered. Stop the pressure, then push the bag down and up sharply to finish.

Repeat for the remaining cupcakes and position a snowflake on top of each cupcake.

FOR 12 CUPCAKES
YOU WILL NEED:

bauble mould (see page 159 for
stockists)

cornflour, for dusting

40g (1½oz) white ready-made
sugar flower paste icing

small paintbrush

edible rainbow dust in gold (see
page 159 for stockists)

boiled water, cooled

edible glitter in gold (see
page 159 for stockists)

piping bag with 5mm (¼ inch)
plain nozzle

1 quantity Vanilla Buttercream
or Cream Cheese Frosting
(see pages 88–9), coloured
with green edible food
colouring paste

12 chocolate or vanilla cupcake
bases (see pages 16 and 66)

CHRISTMAS TREE BAUBLE CUPCAKES

Dust the inside of the mould with a little cornflour. Dab your fingertips into the cornflour to stop them sticking and take a small ball of sugar flower paste icing and press it tightly into the bauble mould. Pop out the shape and repeat until you have 12 baubles.

Using a small dry paintbrush, brush the excess cornflour off the bauble shapes, then leave to set in the refrigerator until hard for a few hours or ideally overnight.

Once set, use a small paintbrush to paint the top of the attaching piece with gold coloured edible rainbow dust. Then lightly brush the bauble base (but not the attachment top) with the cooled boiled water.

Sprinkle edible glitter over the bauble, shake off the excess and leave to dry.

To create the Christmas tree effect, the frosting needs to be free-flowing and not too stiff. Fill the piping bag with frosting, twist the end tightly and squeeze gently until the frosting starts to come through.

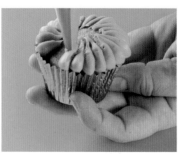

Pipe a dot on the rim of the cupcake, stop squeezing, tip the bag vertically and push the tip of the nozzle towards the centre of the cake. Repeat around the rim, then create a second row in between the gaps and repeat until you reach the middle. Pipe a swirl on top to finish and place a bauble on top.

FOR 12 CUPCAKES
YOU WILL NEED:

cornflour, for dusting

small rolling pin

50g (2oz) green ready-made sugar flower paste icing (see page 159 for stockists)

small sharp knife

small paintbrush with soft bristles

boiled water, cooled

edible glitter in 'disco green', 'yellow' and 'super nova purple' (see page 159 for stockists)

piping bag with a 5mm (¼ inch) plain nozzle

1 quantity Vanilla Buttercream or Cream Cheese Frosting (see pages 88–9), coloured with red, green and/or yellow edible food colouring pastes

12 chocolate or vanilla cupcake bases (see pages 16 and 66)

HOLLY LEAF CUPCAKES

Dust a little cornflour over your work surface to stop the icing from sticking, and roll out the sugar flower paste icing very thinly, about 2mm (¾ inch) thick.

Using the tip of a small sharp knife, carefully cut out 12 holly leaf shapes. (You may find it easier to make a paper template first to cut round.) Leave to dry in the refrigerator for several hours or ideally overnight, until hard.

Using a small paintbrush, lightly brush cooled boiled water over the surface of the holly leaves. Cover with edible glitter and shake off the excess, then leave to dry for a few minutes.

Fill the piping bag with frosting, twist the end tightly and squeeze gently until the frosting starts to come through. Hold the bag vertically and slowly pipe a ring of icing around the edge of a cupcake, then continue in a spiral until you reach the centre and the cupcake is covered. Stop the pressure, then push the bag down and up sharply to finish.

Poke the holly leaf into the top of each cupcake to finish. Repeat with the remaining cupcakes.

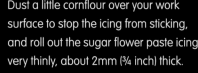

6

NUTTY & CHOCOLATEY CUPCAKES

FRUITY CUPCAKES

RICH & SPICY CUPCAKES

GUILT-FREE CUPCAKES

STYLING CUPCAKES

COOKIES

BARS & BISCUITS

If you are a fan of chewy cookies I can guarantee these will become your new favourite. The combination of the melted toffee pieces, dark chocolate chunks and the freshly-baked cookie dough is so moreish. This is a cookie to eat straight from the oven, ideally with honeycomb ice cream.

DOUBLE CHOCOLATE TOFFEE COOKIES

MAKES 14 COOKIES

150g (5oz) unsalted butter, softened
125g (4oz) soft brown sugar
1 egg
150g (5oz) plain flour
½ tsp baking powder
20g (¾oz) cocoa powder
100g (3½oz) dark chocolate
   chunks or chips
75g (3oz) toffee pieces

Preheat the oven to 200°C/fan 180°C/gas mark 6, and line a flat baking sheet with a silicone mat or baking paper.

In a large bowl, cream the butter and sugar together. Add the egg, then sift in the flour, baking powder and cocoa, and mix until well combined. Fold in the chocolate chunks and toffee pieces.

Place spoonfuls of the mixture on the baking sheet, leaving space between them as they will spread during cooking. Bake for 12–15 minutes, or until golden brown at the edges but still soft in the middle.

Leave to cool on the baking sheet for 5 minutes, then transfer to a wire rack to cool completely.

These fruity-flavoured soft dough cookies will be a hit with everybody, and work perfectly as a festive gift for Christmas if you make them smaller and bag or box them beautifully.

ORANGE & WHITE CHOCOLATE CHIP COOKIES

MAKES ABOUT 36 SMALL COOKIES

125g (4oz) unsalted butter, softened
175g (6oz) caster sugar
2 tsp clear honey
2 tbsp milk
1 tsp vanilla extract
grated zest and juice of 1 orange
250g (8oz) self-raising flour
1 tsp ground cinnamon
100g (3½oz) white chocolate chunks

Preheat the oven to 200°C/fan 180°C/ gas mark 6, and line 2 baking sheets with silicone mats or baking paper.

In a large bowl, cream the butter, sugar and honey together until pale and fluffy. Beat in the milk, vanilla extract, orange zest and juice. Sift the flour and cinnamon together. Mix into the batter, followed by the chocolate chunks.

Place heaped teaspoonfuls of the mixture on the baking sheets, leaving space between them, as they will spread during cooking. Bake for about 10 minutes, or until golden brown at the edges but still soft in the middle.

Leave to cool on the baking sheets for 5 minutes, then transfer to a wire rack to cool completely.

These very traditional Dutch cookies, also known as 'speculaas', are traditionally baked on St Nicholas Eve, 5 December. They make perfect Christmas cookies as you can cut them out into many different shapes and decorate them however you like with royal icing, or keep them simple, as I have here, with a roasted almond topping.

WINDMILL COOKIES

MAKES 40–50 COOKIES, DEPENDING ON SIZE

250g (8oz) unsalted butter, softened
375g (12oz) soft brown sugar
1 egg
½ tsp almond extract
½ tsp vanilla extract
350g (11½oz) plain flour
1 tsp baking powder
½ tsp ground cloves
½ tsp ground cinnamon
½ tsp freshly grated nutmeg
100g (3½oz) finely ground almonds
1 egg, beaten
50g (2oz) flaked almonds

Preheat the oven to 200°C/fan 180°C/gas mark 6, and line several flat baking sheets with silicone mats or baking paper.

In a large bowl, cream the butter and sugar together until pale and fluffy.

Beat in the egg, then stir in the almond and vanilla extracts. Sift the flour, baking powder and spices together. Stir these into the creamed mixture followed by the ground almonds to give a nice smooth dough.

With a rolling pin, roll the dough out on a floured surface to a 5mm (¼ inch) thickness. Using a biscuit cutter, cut out shapes and transfer to the baking sheets. Brush each with beaten egg and sprinkle over the flaked almonds.

Bake for 13–15 minutes, or until nice and golden. Allow them to cool for 5 minutes on the trays before transferring to wire racks to cool completely.

These cookies will keep well in an airtight container.

It is amazing how the flavour of this traditional and iconic cake can be transformed. These chunky soft cookies are bursting with rich cherry and chocolate flavours … the only thing missing is the cream, but I think a drizzle of fresh cream is the perfect accompaniment for these cookies. They're the ideal dessert cookie!

BLACK FOREST SOFT COOKIES

MAKES 12–15

125g (4oz) plain flour
25 (1oz) cocoa powder
1 tsp baking powder
125g (4oz) dark chocolate, broken into pieces
75g (3oz) unsalted butter, softened
100g (3½oz) dark brown sugar
1 large egg
150g (5oz) dried cherries, soaked overnight in 25ml/1fl oz kirsch
150g (5oz) dark chocolate chunks
pouring cream, to serve

Preheat the oven to 200°C/fan 180°C/gas mark 6, and line 3–4 baking sheets with silicone mats or baking paper.

Into a medium bowl, sift the flour, cocoa powder and baking powder.

Melt the dark chocolate in a large heatproof bowl placed over a saucepan of barely simmering water, making sure the bowl does not touch the surface of the water. Leave to cool a little.

In a large bowl, ideally using an electric hand whisk, cream the butter with the sugar until pale and fluffy, then add the egg. Fold in the melted chocolate followed by the sifted dry ingredients, then the drained cherries and the chocolate chunks.

Scoop 1½ tablespoons for each cookie on to the baking sheets, leaving enough space between them to spread during cooking. The mixture will be quite sticky, but this is fine. Press down lightly on each cookie with a fork.

Bake for 18–20 minutes until the cookies are soft, but starting to firm up on top; it's important to remove them from the oven while they are still soft. Leave to cool on the trays for 7–8 minutes, then transfer to wire racks to cool completely. Serve with a drizzle of cream.

If you like chocolate, these cookies will become your 'péché mignon' (indulgence)! They are so rich and chewy, coated with melted marshmallow... what else do you need?

DOUBLE CHOCOLATE & MARSHMALLOW COOKIES

MAKES 24 COOKIES

75g (3oz) plain chocolate, broken into pieces
125g (4oz) unsalted butter, softened
200g (7oz) soft brown sugar
1 egg
4 tbsp milk
1 tsp vanilla extract
150g (5oz) plain flour
100g (3½oz) cocoa powder
1 tsp baking powder
150g (5oz) dark chocolate chunks or chips
75g (3oz) white marshmallows
2 tsp water

Preheat the oven to 200°C/fan 180°C/gas mark 6, and line 2 baking sheets with silicone mats or baking paper.

Melt the chocolate in a heatproof bowl placed over a saucepan of barely simmering water making sure the bowl does not touch the surface of the water. Heat until completely melted and set aside to cool.

In a large bowl, cream the butter and sugar until smooth. Add the egg, milk and vanilla extract, and combine well. Add the cooled melted chocolate and mix again until smooth. Sift in the flour, cocoa and baking powder. Stir in the chocolate chunks or chips.

Place tablespoonfuls of the mixture on the baking sheets, leaving space between them as they will spread during cooking. Flatten them slightly with the back of a spoon that has been dipped in water, and bake for 12 minutes, or until firm to the touch.

Leave to cool on the baking sheets for 5 minutes, then transfer to a wire rack to cool completely.

Place the marshmallows in a small saucepan with the water and melt over a low heat. Drizzle over the cooled cookies.

These delicious, spicy Indian-inspired cookies are full of goodness and flavour.

CHAI TEA COOKIES

MAKES 28 COOKIES

225g (7½oz) unsalted butter, softened
225g (7½oz) soft brown sugar
2 egg yolks
1 tbsp chai tea
½ tsp crushed roasted cardamom seeds
1 tsp vanilla extract
225g (7½oz) wholemeal flour
1 tsp baking powder
110g (3¾oz) rolled oats
100g (3½oz) golden sultanas

Preheat the oven to 200°C/fan 180°C/ gas mark 6, and line 2 baking sheets with silicone mats or baking paper.

In a large bowl, cream the butter and sugar together until light and fluffy. Beat in the egg yolks, chai tea, cardamom seeds and vanilla extract. Sift in the flour and baking powder and tip in the wholemeal left in the sieve, then add the oats. Stir to combine, then fold in the sultanas.

Place spoonfuls of the mixture on the baking sheets, leaving space between them, as they will spread during cooking. Bake for 15 minutes, or until golden brown but still soft in the middle.

Leave to cool on the baking sheets for 5 minutes, then transfer to a wire rack to cool completely.

These nutty cookies are great served with fresh mint tea. Lemon oil can be found in most supermarkets and makes a real difference to the flavour.

LEMON PISTACHIO COOKIES

MAKES 28 COOKIES

100g (3½oz) unsalted butter
 softened
½ tsp grated lemon zest
200g (7oz) golden caster sugar
2 eggs
2 tbsp milk
2 tsp pistachio paste
2 drops of lemon oil
250g (8oz) plain flour
1½ tsp baking powder
50g (2oz) pistachio nuts, shelled
 and roughly chopped
icing sugar, to dust

Preheat the oven to 200°C/fan 180°C/ gas mark 6, and line 2 baking sheets with silicone mats or baking paper.

In a large bowl, blend the butter with lemon zest. Add the sugar and beat well until creamy. Beat in the eggs, milk, pistachio paste and lemon oil, until well combined.

Sift in the flour and baking powder together and fold into the mixture, followed by the pistachio nuts.

Drop teaspoonfuls of the mixture on the baking sheets, spaced well apart, and flatten with the base of a spoon that has been dipped in cold water. Bake for 8–10 minutes, or until lightly golden.

Leave the cookies to cool on the baking sheets for 5 minutes then transfer to a wire rack to cool completely.

Lightly dust with icing sugar just before serving.

I am lucky enough to visit the islands of Hawaii quite often, and my treat there will be anything made with their local macadamia nuts ... these cookies are inspired by this favourite destination.

WHITE CHOCOLATE, MACADAMIA NUT & CRANBERRY COOKIES

MAKES 20 COOKIES

250g (8oz) self-raising flour
175g (6oz) caster sugar
75g (3oz) whole rolled oats
125g (4oz) unsalted butter
2 tbsp golden syrup
2 tbsp milk
100g (3½oz) white chocolate broken into pieces
100g (3½oz) macadamia nuts, roughly chopped
50g (2oz) dried cranberries
vanilla ice cream and golden syrup, to serve

Preheat the oven to 200°C/fan 180°C/ gas mark 6, and line 2 baking sheets with a silicone mat or baking paper.

In a large bowl, mix the flour, sugar and oats. Rub the butter into the flour (like making a short crust pastry) until it looks like a crumble topping. Add the golden syrup and milk, and combine together. Stir in the white chocolate, nuts and cranberries.

Place spoonfuls of the mixture on the baking sheets, leaving space between them, as they will spread during cooking. Flatten the cookies slightly with a spoon that has been dipped in cold water. Bake for 15 minutes, or until golden brown.

These cookies are amazing served with vanilla ice cream with a drizzle of golden syrup.

7

My friend Laury, who is obsessed with anything Italian, introduced me to this recipe. She bakes them in the build-up to Thanksgiving and also serves them with a spicy Christmas coffee, just to put you in the mood.

PUMPKIN BISCOTTI

MAKES APPROXIMATELY 60

100g peeled pumpkin flesh, cut
    into 2.5 cm (1-inch) cubes
25g (1oz) unsalted butter
200g (7oz) toasted pecan nuts,
    coarsely chopped
450g (14½oz) plain flour
350g (11½oz) brown sugar
2 tsp baking powder
2 tsp mixed spice
2 large eggs, lightly beaten
1 tbsp vanilla extract

Steam the pumpkin for 15–20 minutes until soft, then leave to drain in a sieve over a bowl to remove as much moisture as possible. Then mash or purée and allow to cool.

Preheat the oven to 200°C/fan 180°C/ gas mark 6, and line 2 baking sheets with silicone mats or baking paper.

Melt the butter in a frying pan and add the pecan nuts. Cook, stirring constantly, until nuts are lightly browned. Remove from the heat, and leave to cool.

Meanwhile, in a large bowl combine the flour, sugar, baking powder and mixed spice. In another bowl, combine the pumpkin, eggs and vanilla extract, stirring well with a wire whisk. Slowly add the pumpkin mixture to the flour mixture, stirring until the dry ingredients are moistened. (The mixture will initially be very crumbly, but will gradually become moist after stirring.) Add the nuts to the mixture and stir in.

Turn the mixture out on a lightly floured surface and, with lightly floured hands, divide it into 6 portions and shape each into a 30cm (12 inch) long, slightly flattened log. Place these about 7cm (3 inches) apart on the baking sheets.

Bake for 25 minutes, then remove from the oven and leave the logs to cool for 15 minutes.

Using a serrated knife, cut each log across into 1cm (½ inch) slices. Place these on baking sheets lined with a silicone mat or baking paper, and bake for another 15 minutes. Allow to cool completely on wire rack before serving.

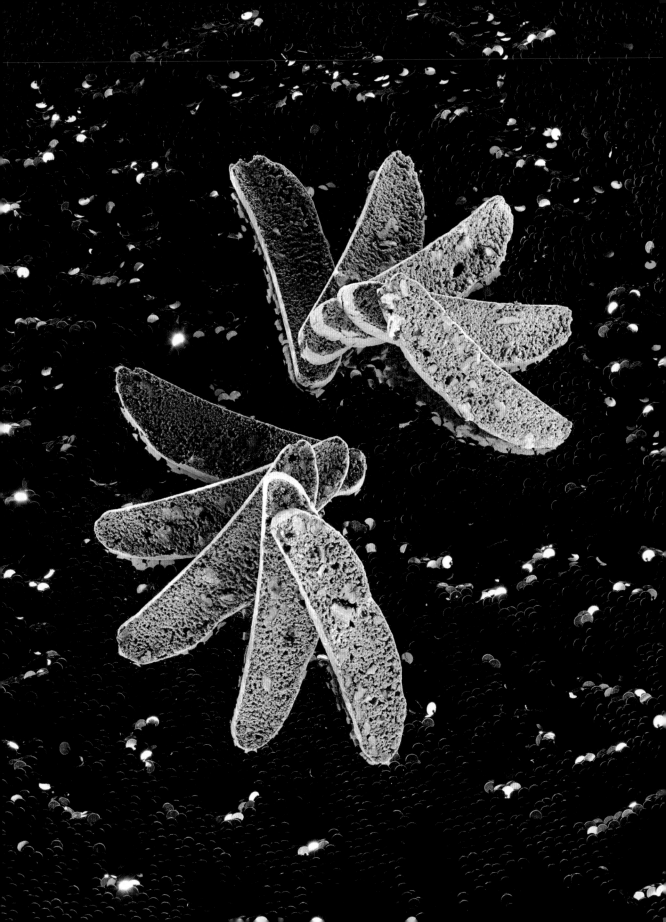

I was very sceptical about my friend Paul Feig's brownie recipe but after tasting them I am a complete convert! The rich chocolate flavour is boosted by the espresso, and the crystallized ginger cuts right through the sweetness.

ESPRESSO BROWNIES WITH CRYSTALLIZED GINGER

MAKES 12 BROWNIES

200g (7oz) dark chocolate, broken into pieces
200g (7oz) unsalted butter
4 eggs
200g (7oz) golden caster sugar
2 tbsp espresso or very strong instant coffee
200g (200g) plain flour, sifted
75g (3oz) crystallized stem ginger, chopped

Preheat the oven to 200°C/fan 180°C/gas mark 6, and line a 25 x 20cm (10 x 8 inch) baking tin with buttered baking paper.

Place the chocolate and butter in a large heatproof bowl over a saucepan of barely simmering water, making sure the bowl does not touch the surface of the water. Heat, stirring until smooth and completely melted. Remove from the heat and half-cool.

In a large bowl, beat the eggs and sugar, ideally with an electric hand whisk, until pale. Beat in the espresso followed by the half-cooled chocolate mixture. Fold in the flour followed by the ginger.

Pour this batter into the tin and bake for 20–25 minutes, or until crusty on top but still slightly gooey inside. Leave to cool in the tin. When cool, cut into bars.

These very light, chewy treats are great for kids to make and eat. They are also always a big hit for a school bake sale.

MARSHMALLOW RICE BARS

MAKES 24 SQUARES

50g (2oz) unsalted butter, plus extra
   for greasing
200g (7oz) white marshmallows
150g (5oz) crisped rice cereal

FOR THE TOPPING
50g (2oz) white marshmallows
4 tsp water
50g (2oz) pink marshmallows
75g (3oz) white chocolate, melted

In a large saucepan, melt the butter over a low heat. Add the marshmallows and stir until these are melted and well blended in. Cook for 2 minutes longer, stirring constantly. Remove from the heat. When the mixture is cool, stir in the cereal until it is all well coated.

Butter a 30 x 20cm (12 x 8-inch) tin. Using a buttered spatula or sheet of greaseproof paper, press the mixture evenly and firmly into the prepared tin.

To make the topping: in a small saucepan, melt the white marshmallows with 2 teaspoons of water over a gentle heat, stirring. Drizzle this mixture over the top of the cereal layer. Repeat this step with the pink marshmallows. Finally drizzle the melted white chocolate over the top to finish.

Chill until set, then cut into 5cm (2-inch) squares and serve.

Sponge fingers have been around for centuries. Light and delicious, they have long been a favourite of Parisian ladies to accompany their flutes of Champagne. In fact, these raspberry versions are a perfect accompaniment to rosé Champagne. Clink, clink!

RASPBERRY SPONGE FINGERS

MAKES 30–35 FINGER BISCUITS

4 eggs, separated
150g (5oz) golden caster sugar
a few drops of pink food colouring
2 drops of natural raspberry
    flavouring
100g (3½oz) flour
½ tsp baking powder
icing sugar, to dust

Preheat the oven to 200°C/fan 180°C/ gas mark 6, and line two 45 x 30cm (18 x 12-inch) baking sheets with silicone mats or baking paper.

In a large and scrupulously clean bowl, beat the egg whites, ideally using an electric hand whisk on high, until they form soft peaks. Slowly add 2 tablespoons of the sugar and continue beating until stiff and glossy.

In another bowl, beat the egg yolks with the remaining sugar until thick and very pale in colour. (The use of an electric hand whisk really helps to get a good result here.) Add the pink food colouring and raspberry flavouring to the mixture.

Sift the flour and baking powder together. Fold half the egg whites into the egg yolk mixture, then fold in the flour, followed by the remaining egg whites, taking care not to knock out too much of the air that you have painstakingly beaten in.

Transfer the mixture to a piping bag fitted with a 1.5cm (¾ inch) plain piping nozzle. Pipe the mixture on the prepared baking sheets in about 7cm (3-inch) lengths, leaving a 4cm (1½-inch) space between them. Liberally dust with icing sugar, leave to rest for 2 minutes, then dust again.

Bake in the oven for about 8 minutes until golden brown. Leave to cool on the sheets for 5 minutes before transferring to wire racks to cool completely.

These delicious treats are good for the health-conscious as are they packed with goodness and will give you that vavavoom you need to start the day.

OAT & FRUIT BAR WITH YOGHURT TOPPING

MAKES 10 BARS

2 tbsp sunflower seeds
2 tbsp pumpkin seeds
2 tbsp linseeds
100g (3½oz) unsalted butter
3 tbsp golden syrup
2 bananas, peeled and mashed
150g (5oz) rolled oats
150g (5oz) dried mixed fruit

FOR THE YOGHURT TOPPING
125g (4oz) icing sugar, sieved
40ml (1½fl oz) natural yoghurt

Preheat the oven to 200°C/fan 180°C/ gas mark 6. Grease a 20cm (8-inch) square shallow tin and line the base with baking paper.

Roughly chop all the seeds.

Melt the butter in a saucepan and stir in the golden syrup. Add the chopped seeds and mashed bananas, together with the rolled oats and dried fruit. Mix together well.

Spoon the mixture into the prepared tin and level the surface. Bake for about 30 minutes or until golden brown. Leave to cool in the tin.

To make the Yoghurt Topping: mix the icing sugar with the yoghurt. If it is too thick, add a little more yoghurt.

Drizzle on top of the cooled oat bars. Leave to set and cut into squares and then into triangles with a sharp knife.

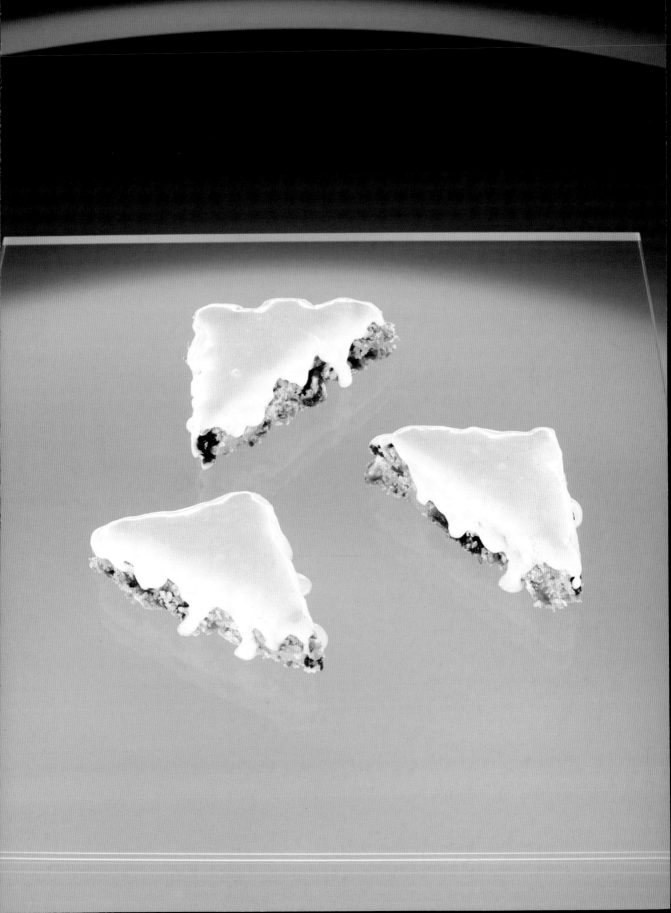

This classic shortbread recipe is perfect for making iced or decorated biscuits. The technique here is to use layers of ready-made coloured easy-roll icing, but you can pipe them with royal icing, too. By making a little hole in them as they come out of the oven you can turn them into hanging ornaments for Christmas or other occasions. The exact baking time will depend on the size and final shape of your biscuits, so keep and eye on them whilst cooking. When using sugar flower paste, always remember to cover it with clingfilm when not using, as it dries out very rapidly.

ICED SHORTBREAD BISCUITS

MAKES 36–40 COOKIES, DEPENDING ON SIZE

300g (10oz) unsalted butter
500g (1lb) plain flour
150g (5oz) caster sugar
1 egg
2 tsp milk
1 tsp vanilla extract

FOR THE ICING
250g (8oz) ready-made sugar
    flower paste in a selection
    of colours (see page 159
    for stockists)
75g (3oz) cornflour
50g (2oz) sieved apricot jam,
    warmed

Preheat the oven to 200°C/fan 180°C/gas mark 6, and line 2 flat baking sheets with silicone mats or baking paper.

Rub the butter into the flour, add the other ingredients and work them in until they bind together to form a nice smooth dough. Don't over-knead it!

Roll the dough out on a floured surface to a thickness of about 5mm (¼ inch). Using pastry cutters, cut out your favourite shapes. Re-roll the trimmings and cut out more shapes.

Place the biscuits on the baking sheets and bake them in the centre of the oven for 12–15 minutes (see note above), or until they are light golden in colour.

To ice the bicuits, roll out the sugar flower paste as thinly as possible, dusting it with the cornflour to prevent it from sticking.

Cut out your chosen shapes from the sheet of icing. Brush the apricot jam over each cookie and gently place a layer of icing on top. Use a small brush dipped in boiling water to secure layers of icing together.

These little French treats are a good alternative to biscuits or cookies. You can top them with any dried fruits and nuts. I like mine exotic-looking and glamorous, so flakes of gold leaf are a must.

WHITE CHOCOLATE MENDIANTS

MAKES ABOUT 18

200g (7oz) good-quality white
    chocolate, broken into pieces
150g (5oz) assorted dried exotic
    fruits and nuts
a few flakes of edible gold leaf,
    to decorate (optional)

Line a large baking sheet with baking paper.

Gently melt the chocolate in a heatproof bowl over a saucepan of barely simmering water, making sure the bowl does not touch the surface of the water.

Place teaspoonfuls of the chocolate on the paper and smooth into 5cm (2-inch) circles. Working quickly, sprinkle over the dried fruits and nuts, and flake over the gold leaf.

Leave for at least 30 minutes in the refrigerator to set.

These are delicious served warm with crème fraîche and a drizzle of maple syrup. Always use pure maple syrup, not flavoured syrup or Mr Cox will beat you up!

MAPLE PECAN STICKY BARS

MAKES 12

FOR THE FILLING
175g (6oz) pecan nuts, roughly chopped
100ml (3½fl oz) pure maple syrup
200g (7oz) soft brown sugar
2 tbsp whipping cream
150g (5oz) unsalted butter
½ tsp vanilla extract

FOR THE SHORTCRUST BASE
100g (3½oz) unsalted butter, softened, plus more for greasing
75g (3oz) golden caster sugar
1 egg yolk
175g (6oz) plain flour

Preheat the oven to 200°C/fan 180°C/gas mark 6, and butter a 23 x 23 x 5cm (9 x 9 x 2-inch) square cake tin.

Toast the pecan nuts in the oven for 5 minutes and leave to cool.

To make the shortcrust base: ideally using a free-standing electric mixer in a bowl, beat together the butter, sugar and egg yolk until blended. Add the flour and beat until a soft dough is formed. Gather the dough together and press it into the bottom of the tin and 2cm (¾ inch) up the sides. Bake for about 18–20 minutes, or until golden. Remove from the oven, but leave the oven on. Leave to cool and form a crust whilst you make the filling.

To make the filling: in a medium saucepan, combine all the ingredients except the nuts and vanilla extract. Bring to the boil, stirring until the butter melts and the mixture is smooth. Boil for 30 seconds. Remove from the heat, then mix in the nuts and vanilla extract.

Pour the hot filling over the cooled crust, and bake for about 15 minutes more until the filling is bubbling in the centre.

Allow to cool completely in the tin when the filling will become firm, then chill in the refrigerator for at least 1 hour and up to 2 hours.

When chilled, cut into bars with a large sharp knife.

The combination here of the salted peanuts and the dark chocolate works really very well and the frosting makes these brownies very rich and indulgent. I like cutting them into bite-sized pieces… a good excuse to eat more of them!

PEANUT BUTTER & FUDGE BROWNIES

MAKES ABOUT 20 BROWNIES, DEPENDING ON SIZE

175g (6oz) unsalted butter
300g (10oz) dark chocolate, broken into pieces
350g (11½oz) golden caster sugar
1½ tsp vanilla extract
4 large eggs
100g (3½oz) plain flour
175g (6oz) roasted salted peanuts, coarsely chopped

FOR THE FROSTING

225g (7½oz) chunky peanut butter
100g (3½oz) unsalted butter, softened
150g (5oz) icing sugar
1 tbsp milk
1 tsp vanilla extract

FOR THE GANACHE

75g (3oz) dark chocolate, broken into pieces
icing sugar, to dust

Preheat the oven to 200°C/fan 180°C/gas mark 6, and line a 33 x 23 x 5cm (13 x 9 x 2 inch) baking tin with foil or baking paper.

Place the butter and chocolate in a large saucepan and stir them over a low heat until they are melted and smooth. Remove from the heat.

Whisk in the sugar and vanilla extract, followed by the eggs, one at a time. Then fold in the flour followed by the nuts.

Spread the mixture in the prepared tin and bake for 25–30 minutes until a skewer inserted into centre comes out with moist crumbs attached. Leave to cool in the tin.

To make the Frosting; in a medium bowl, ideally using an electric mixer, beat the peanut butter with half the ordinary butter until blended. Then beat in the icing sugar, followed by the milk and vanilla extract. Spread the frosting over the cooled brownies.

To make the Ganache; melt the dark chocolate with the remaining butter in a heatproof bowl over a saucepan of simmering water, making sure the bowl does not touch the surface of the water. Allow to cool slightly, then drizzle over the top. Dust with icing sugar before cutting into squares.

These old-fashioned biscuits are perfect with tea or coffee. The combination of the rye flour and the molasses gives them a rich taste and the melted fudge provides a lovely sticky marbled effect.

MOLASSES CRINKLES

MAKES 28 BISCUITS

175g (6oz) unsalted butter, softened
225g (7½oz) soft brown sugar
1 egg
50g (2oz) molasses
150g (5oz) rye flour
2 tsp baking powder
¼ tsp salt
½ tsp ground cloves
1 tsp ground cinnamon
1 tsp ground ginger
125g (4oz) fudge pieces
2 tbsp granulated sugar, for dipping

In a large bowl, ideally using an electric hand whisk, mix together the butter, sugar, egg and molasses.

In another bowl, blend together the flour, baking powder, salt and spices. Gradually add this to the butter mixture, followed by the fudge pieces. Chill in the refrigerator for 20 minutes.

Preheat the oven to 200°C/fan 180°C/gas mark 6, and line 1 or 2 baking sheets with baking paper.

Roll the chilled dough in your hands to make 3cm (1¼-inch) balls.

Dip their tops in the sugar and place them, sugar side up, 7.5cm (3¼ inches) apart on the baking sheets.

Bake for 10–12 minutes, or until just set but not hard. Allow the biscuits to cool on the sheets before removing.

These are said to be the national sweet of Canada! I like eating these moreish bars at room temperature as they are then creamier and richer.

NANAIMO BARS

MAKES 10 BARS

FOR THE FIRST LAYER
65g (2½oz) sugar
15g (½oz) cocoa, sifted
125g (4oz) digestive biscuit crumbs
65g (2½oz) desiccated coconut
65g (2½oz) walnuts, finely
    chopped
125g (4oz) unsalted butter, melted

FOR THE SECOND LAYER
50g (2oz) butter, softened
25g (1oz) custard powder
250g (8oz) icing sugar
a little warm water (optional)

FOR THE THIRD LAYER
150g (5oz) dark chocolate, broken
    into pieces
50g (2oz) unsalted butter

Line a shallow 20cm (8-inch) square baking tin with baking paper.

To make the first layer: in a large bowl, mix all the ingredients together except the butter. Pour the melted butter over and combine well. Using a spoon, press this into the tin and chill in the refrigerator for 15 minutes to set.

To make the second layer: cream the butter with the custard powder, ideally with an electric hand whisk, until fluffy. Then add the icing sugar a little at a time. Add a little warm water if it gets too stiff. Smooth the creamy mixture on top of the set biscuit base, and again place in the refrigerator for 15 minutes to set.

To make the third layer: melt the chocolate and butter in a heatproof bowl over a saucepan of simmering water until smooth and glossy, making sure the base of the bowl does not touch the water. Let it cool slightly, then pour over the custard layer and smooth with a palette knife. Chill for a further 15 minutes, or until set.

Take out of the refrigerator 30 minutes before serving to allow it to soften slightly, then cut into bars with a large sharp knife.

Blue Ribbons Sugarcraft Centre
29 Walton Road
East Molesey
Surrey KT8 0DH
www.blueribbons.co.uk
Tel. +44 (0)20 8941 1591

*Stockist of rose-shaped
silicone rubber push moulds;
edible food colouring pastes;
edible rainbow dust and glitter;
edible confectioners' glaze and
sugar decorations including
diamonds and flowers.*

Cake Craft Shop
7 Chatterton Road
Bromley
Kent BR2 9QW
www.cakecraftshop.co.uk
Tel. +44 (0)1732 463573

*Stockist of edible food colouring
pastes; edible glaze spray and
sugar decorations and flowers.*

FPC Sugarcraft
www.fpcsugarcraft.co.uk
Tel. +44 (0)117 9853249

*Supplier of lacy undies, rose,
skull, bauble, beach bum and
torso-shaped silicone rubber
moulds. Available online only.*

**Jane Asher Party Cakes
& Sugarcraft**
22–24 Cale Street
London SW3 3QU
www.janeasher.com
Tel. +44 (0)20 7584 6177

*Shop and online store selling
edible food colouring pastes;
edible rainbow dust and glitters;
flavourings; sugar flower paste
and ready-made icings;
confectioners' glaze; piping gel;
edible gold leaf and decorations*

Squires Kitchen
3 Waverley Lane
Farnham
Surrey GU9 8BB
www.squires-shop.com
Tel. +44 (0)1252 260260

*Shop and online store selling
silicone rubber push moulds;
snowflake, flower and holly
leaf-shaped plunger cutters;
chocolate paste; sugar flower
paste and ready-made icings;
edible gold leaf and edible
confectioners' glaze.*

The Sugar Craft Shop
The Bread Basket
1 Elm Road
Stonehouse
Gloucestershire GL10 2NP
www.thesugarcraftshop.co.uk
Tel. +44 (0)1453 822709

*Shop and online store selling
edible food colouring pastes;
piping gel and sugar flower
paste icing.*

USEFUL CONTACTS

ACKNOWLEDGEMENTS

Thanks to my mom for her baking and getting me hooked on cookies and cakes.

To Elizabeth Hurley for introducing me to Eric who has made my wilder dreams taste better than I could ever imagine.

A special thanks to Elton and David for writing the kind foreword to this book.

I would also like to thank our wonderful teams in the shop and bakery. Their boundless enthusiasm and hard work has been a big part of Cox Cookies & Cake's success.

Patrick Cox

Thank you to my first teachers Hervé Le Grand and Albert Roux – generous-hearted chefs who were happy to share their passion and their recipes … a spirit I hope to continue with my books and in my own Cookery School at Cake Boy.

To Paul for his unconditional support.

To Elizabeth for the introduction, and to Patrick for inviting me to join him on this exciting journey.

To all the staff at Cox Cookies & Cake and Cake Boy, and to Anne Kibel and Jean Egbunike.

To Rachel Wood and Wendy Lee for testing all our yummy recipes.

To Sybella, Juliette and Jonathan for making this book so special.

To Becca – nice to work together again and I'm looking forward to the next project.

And finally a big thank you to Patrick Llewlyn-Davies for the amazing photography of the cakes.

Eric Lanlard